LaVell

LaVell

airing it out

LaVell Edwards
with Lee Benson

SHADOW MOUNTAIN
SALT LAKE CITY, UTAH

Library of Congress Cataloging-in-Publication Data

Edwards, LaVell.
  LaVell : airing it out / LaVell Edwards with Lee Benson.
    p.   cm.
  ISBN 1-57345-068-5 (hardbound)
  1. Edwards, LaVell. 2. Football coaches—United States—
Biography. 3. Brigham Young University—Football—History.
I. Benson, Lee, 1948–   . II. Title.
  GV939.E43A3   1995
  796.332'07'092—dc20
  [B]   95-23342
                                                                CIP

Printed in the United States of America

10   9   8   7   6   5   4   3   2   1

To Patti, Ann, John, and Jimmy,
who have made it all possible . . .
and worthwhile.

We could do it again, but it wouldn't be no better.

—WILLIE NELSON

CONTENTS

Grateful appreciation is due many individuals who contributed in a variety of ways to this project and who gave freely of their time and resources. Certainly the book would have met a premature demise without the uncanny and often mysterious talents of Shirley Johnson, the invaluable BYU football office secretary who knows everything and everyone and who, in another life, ought to be either a private investigator, a personal secretary to a rock star, or the director of the CIA. Equally valuable was the uniquely insightful editing of Ann Edwards Cannon, who did her work in a closet until LaVell and Patti's five grandsons found her.

Those willing to share observations in one form or another make an extensive list, including Don L. "Sanky" Dixon, Dick Felt, Chris Pella, Lance Reynolds, Grant Teaff, Johnny Majors, Dick Tomey, Ted Tollner, Rich Brooks, Jim Walden, Vince Dooley, Dick MacPherson, Paul Roach, Ron McBride, Steve Young, Gifford Nielsen, Chuck Cutler, Glen Kozlowski, Patti Edwards, Ann Edwards Cannon, John Edwards, and Jimmy Edwards. To these individuals, none of whom went "off the record" so much as to clear their throats, many thanks.

The publication staff at Deseret Book Company, in particular vice-president Sheri Dew, who conceived the project; Jay Parry, who edited the manuscript; and Michelle Eckersley, who designed the book and the cover, have been a pleasure to work with, and their work has been invaluable.

Lastly, thanks goes to all the players and

coaches at Brigham Young University, and to all the fans in the stands, from 1962 onward. It's their synergism that forms the very heart of this book.

W hen you consider the good fortune LaVell Edwards has enjoyed as a major college football coach, it's little wonder that his first book would be a whole lot about the game he has loved and coached so successfully for so many years.

Football is in LaVell's blood. It always has been, and he shows no signs of wanting to get away from it anytime soon. When the weather cools and the leaves start to change, LaVell responds to some basic instinct that can apparently be satisfied only by the cadence of a quarterback calling out his signals, the sound of a football being punted, and the grunting of the players as they practice blocking and tackling. I think we're a lot alike in the way we respond to the sounds and smells and sights of college football.

So it's no surprise that when he got around to writing a book, football would be a major part of it. After all, from the time he was a grade-schooler and would stop by the high school to watch football practice through the fence, right down to the time of his team's appearance in the 1994 Copper Bowl, there has never been a football season where he hasn't been involved in the game—either as an observer, a player, or a coach.

And with all those years of successful coaching at Brigham Young University and perennial conference championships and annual post-season bowl appearances and an unparalleled succession of All-American quarterbacks and a Heisman Trophy winner and a national championship to show for it, football has been a major part of the fabric of LaVell's life.

LaVell could probably sell a huge number of copies of his book to coaches alone if they thought it contained the secret of his remarkable success. But this is not only a book about coaching strategies and the intricacies of the passing game. Beyond football, it is a book about life and values and family and faith. On those topics, LaVell is more than qualified to write a book.

In a way, LaVell's experience as a player foreshadowed his coaching style. He was a lineman, who did most of his bleeding in anonymity and with little fanfare. Now, during games he stands stoically on the sidelines, his facial expression revealing nothing of what may be going through his mind. (Karl Tucker, the longtime golf coach at BYU, has said of him, "LaVell's happy—he just forgot to tell his face.") He seldom gets agitated, even when the referee's call goes against him. Looking at him, you can't tell if his team is ahead by forty points (as they often are) or behind with time running out. That serenity is probably the product of LaVell's certainty about what matters most in life.

He has managed to avoid many of the occupational hazards of his profession—petty jealousies and feuds and grudges. If he has enemies, they've resented him in silence, and I've never met one. Maybe one reason he is universally admired and liked, even by rival coaches, is the way his teams beat you. With their passing attack, it can happen so quickly it's almost painless. Before you know it, you've been skewered, and LaVell's at midfield, shaking your hand, patting your back, and telling you what a great football team you've got.

In winning his two hundredth game as a coach, LaVell joined a pretty exclusive club. But when you consider that his career has never been marred by recruiting scandals or NCAA sanctions, and that he's been loyal to BYU, passing up more lucrative offers to coach in other places, and that he enjoys the friendship and respect of former players and even rival coaches, he's accomplished something even more remarkable in the annals of modern, major-college football. When it comes to integrity and loyalty, he belongs to an even more exclusive club.

I admire and respect LaVell Edwards for his successful program and all that he has accomplished professionally. He represents everything good that should be implied in the title of "coach."

But more than that, I have been proud to have him call me a friend.

—Joe Paterno
Head coach,
Pennsylvania State University

I was eighteen years old and more nervous than I'd ever been. I was on my recruiting visit to the BYU campus in Provo, Utah, a world away from my hometown in Connecticut. All the potential recruits for that spring weekend were lined up in Shirley Johnson's office, waiting to go into the Big Kahuna's office—LaVell's. There wasn't a steady knee in the room.

I remember I was the last because I was Young, right at the end of the alphabet. By the time it was my turn I went in and met a coach who was by then a very famous person. As I sat down in the chair in front of his desk, I was in awe of the man who was speaking to me. I was excited about the possibility of actually being able to play for him, silently praying he would offer me a scholarship. He told me of the large number of kids who wanted to come to BYU. He said there were never enough scholarships to go around. He said he'd looked at my game films and appreciated my talent. I didn't know what he was going to say next. I was afraid that this late in the day his scholarship quota might be all tapped out.

Then he leaned back in that big chair of his, locked his hands behind his neck, and looked out the window . . . and I was sure he'd fallen asleep. But he hadn't fallen asleep; he was just reflecting. After I had suffered a few minutes of agony, he opened his eyes and declared that he had a scholarship for me.

I have often wondered since just how in the world he could have known that this kid in front of him, who had never played quarterback the way BYU played quarterback—who would drop back to pass for literally the first time in his life the upcoming fall when he was a freshman at BYU—could one day actually make it.

I think that story embodies LaVell Edwards' greatest quality. He has a tremendous ability to understand people and visualize what they can become. So much of what he does, he does with feel. A great deal of feel.

When he leaned back in his chair that day in his office, it was D-Day for me. D-Day in the sense of what was going to happen to me. He could see things I couldn't. No matter what anyone says, I wasn't a big recruit. I came with no guarantees. But he leaned back and said, You know what, I like this kid. I think he can be something. I don't know what just yet, but I think he can be something.

It was my good fortune to run into what I believe is one of the great people-skilled persons in the world. It is a God-given talent that LaVell Edwards has. It is something he was blessed with. You can't learn it. It's a sixth sense that very few people have. I think a lot of people miss the real LaVell Edwards when they focus on his folksy style, with his dry sense of humor and his lack of outward emotion. I think they misinterpret his great ability to relate to people. He's a people person. He understands people. That's why he was able to take a Jim McMahon and a Giff Nielsen, to name two of the wide variety of personalities he's seen come through the building, and have both of them not only successfully play for him but also respect him. That is not easy.

Football is the most demanding people-oriented profession in the world. I truly believe that. I've tried to look at all professions and I haven't found one that relies more on people skills. The diversity that football brings, the number of people you need to put together under stressful circumstances—it all comes down to people working with people.

You couldn't have chosen a better profession for LaVell Edwards than football. You couldn't have found a better arena for him to be able to assess personalities and work with people in a way that generates not only success but mutual respect. (Believe me, a guy who's made his life in football: there are very few people in the business who have that kind of respect.) If you don't see that as LaVell's greatest quality, if you don't recognize him for that unique ability, then you've missed him at his greatness.

I think you'll find that most guys who have played for LaVell have a story like mine. The vast majority of the time it's been LaVell who's had that sense of where to put the pieces when no one else was quite as clear. It was true for me when he decided to put me on the team and it was true when assistant coach Ted Tollner walked in a year later and said to him, "I think this kid needs to get another shot at quarterback." LaVell leaned back in his chair again, he thought about it for another moment, and then he said, "All right, let's do that." It was a simple answer that had gone through a very complex brain, a brain that has that ability to break it all down and make the right decisions.

The problem is there aren't many people like him in the world. I've been around. If I could find another guy like that I would run to him to have him coach me.

He has the skills to see deeper, to penetrate, to visually stand in the other person's shoes and see and feel things from his or her perspective. He brings a lot of troubled kids into the program, a lot of unique personalities, a lot of diversity, and he's able to relate to each individual and bring out his best. To me, he's a one-in-a-billion type of person. Maybe I'm wrong. But I'm convinced I'd be selling stock right now if not for LaVell Edwards.

Luckily, BYU football got him, because whatever he decided to do he would have been able to put people together and it would have been successful. It would have worked. He would have won. Truly, if a company could hire LaVell to run its management team, it would find skyrocketing sales. You can say all you want about offensive schemes and the passing game and all that other stuff. I don't care what LaVell chose to do, it would have worked. Because he can take the farmer kid from Idaho, the city kid from L.A., the troubled kid from Salt Lake City, and the kid from Connecticut whose bishop keeps calling, and he can figure out how to bring them all together and turn them into a team.

—STEVE YOUNG
SAN FRANCISCO FORTY-NINERS

To anyone who even remotely knows LaVell Edwards this will come as no surprise: This book was not his idea. The project actually had quite a roundabout start when Sheri Dew, vice-president at Deseret Book, was attending Education Week classes at Brigham Young University in the summer of 1993. During one session she heard a presentation from several BYU football coaches who kept the audience enthralled with "LaVell stories."

The experience was an education for Sheri, who came away thinking what a lot of other people have thought over the years: Someone ought to write these things down. LaVell Edwards is no ordinary man.

Being unconventional isn't something LaVell Edwards works at. It comes as natural to him as everything else he does. He is without pretense, and for that reason the idea of writing his own book had never crossed his mind. A forward pass on first down? Yes, that had occurred to him. But not a book.

At first he balked at the idea, but he warmed to the possibility when it was pointed out to him that a lot of people have been curious for a long time as to just how he was able to produce a championship football program out of what was once the college football equivalent of flying standby. From time to time he said he'd wondered the same thing. Putting it down on paper might help make it clearer in his own mind.

The idea of writing a book that was more memoir than autobiography was also appealing, with Arthur Ashe's critically acclaimed memoir,

Days of Grace, serving as a prototype. In *Days of Grace* Ashe used his life story as a springboard to give insight into his feelings, principles, and philosophies on a variety of subjects ranging from AIDS to race to apartheid to Wimbledon.

LaVell liked that concept and, to that end, collected his own thoughts on subjects of his choosing, to be found in the pages that follow. They range from his penchant for delegation to observations on relationships to football philosophy to the evolution of the BYU passing game. He talks about how and why he does things.

For a person not used to giving advice, or lecturing much at all about anything, the process wasn't as natural for LaVell as, say, hitting a five iron, but in the end he proved up to the task.

The only thing he couldn't do was tell the "LaVell stories" that Sheri Dew was so enamored of in the first place. Which is understandable. LaVell Edwards telling LaVell Edwards stories would be tantamount to Ben Hogan telling Ben Hogan stories, or John Wooden telling John Wooden stories, or, if he were still alive, Bear Bryant telling Bear Bryant stories. For that reason, between the chapters of the book are insights into LaVell Edwards as related by coaches, players, family members, and others. A few "LaVell stories," in other words.

These stories were not hard to come by. Getting people to talk about LaVell Edwards was not a problem. I contacted a wide range of sources, among them some of the very pillars of college football and, to my surprise after years of being accustomed—in my capacity as a newspaper writer—to waiting weeks, months, sometimes years for returned calls, found that most of the time my calls, once the subject was established, were returned within the hour.

People without pretense don't make enemies, and even in a business where competition is fierce and bad blood can often be as near as one touchdown too many, it is perhaps LaVell Edwards' finest legacy that if he has enemies, they are living in another galaxy. His friendships cross all the barriers and all personality types. He is as close to Fresno State's Jim Sweeney as he is to Utah's Ron McBride, to name two coaching personalities at opposite ends of the spectrum.

He has won over two hundred games—a plateau he topped early last season as he became only the fourteenth coach in major college football history to do so. As of this writing, only eight major college coaches have won more games (their names are Bear Bryant, Pop Warner, Amos Alonzo Stagg, Joe Paterno, Bobby Bowden, Woody Hayes, Bo Schembechler, and Tom Osborne) and he could yet catch two or three of them. He is credited with modernizing the forward pass in the college game. The 77–12 record his teams compiled during a seven-year stretch from 1979 through 1985, which accounted for seven consecutive conference championships and the 1984 national championship, stands as one of the most prolific runs in NCAA Division I football history. In two-plus decades his teams have averaged nine wins a year.

He has coached twenty-five first team All-Americans, among them four Davey O'Brien Award winners, two Outland Trophy winners, and one Heisman Trophy winner. If you think it's easy having players run the awards spectrum from top quarterback to top lineman to the nation's most outstanding player, check how many other coaches in college history have had players win even one of each of those honors. (The answer is four: Joe Paterno, Dennis Erickson, Barry Switzer, and Fred Akers, and none has a grand total as high as seven.) During a stretch from 1980 through 1992 he had a former player represented on the Super Bowl winning team every single season. Overall his teams have won sixteen conference championships and have gone to nineteen bowl games, including seventeen in a row through the 1994 season.

And yet, people have no problem at all talking about LaVell Edwards as if they'd lived next door to him all their lives—and borrowed his tools.

He is as approachable as a bellman. Others feel free to enjoy his quirks because he enjoys them as well. This is a man whose assistant coaches would try to trick "in the old days" when the score was soaring out of sight and they still wanted more. Since LaVell never wears a headset, they knew that to be able to give the order to pull the starting quarterback and back off on the passing plays, he had to first track down the graduate assistant who was relaying information from the press box to the field. When the coaches in the press box would see LaVell down on the sidelines start looking around for the G.A.—and they knew that look—they'd tell the G.A. where to hide: behind the water cooler, behind a large offensive lineman, and so forth, so LaVell couldn't find him. Usually they could maneuver the G.A. away from the coach for at least another series or two, and one or two more touchdowns.

Well, okay, they tell the story anonymously. But they still tell it.

There have been few coaches who have demonstrated more loyalty, both to those they coach for and those they coach with. Certainly no one has ever coached on the major college level and fired fewer people than LaVell Edwards has. In more than two decades he's never fired anybody. His staff has continuity like the Ming dynasty's.

This is not a book of controversy. No vengeance, no getting even, very little conflict and turmoil. No one gets ridiculed. No one gets maligned. No one gets trashed. And, as you might note, neither does anyone get particularly glorified.

In many regards LaVell is still anonymous, shadowed by the Rocky Mountains, the Mountain Time Zone, and BYU's austere football past. In many regards it is only within the inner sanctums of the college game that LaVell Edwards gets his full due. There, and in the Cougar Club, of course. But by anyone's standards he is a coaching anomaly, one who has found stability and success without sacrificing anything at all, principles included. A rare breed, indeed. This is a coach of whom the NCAA infractions department says "LaVell who?"; whose wife says, "I still get goose bumps every time I hear his car pull in the driveway"; and whose assistant coaches, many of whom have been around since long before anyone in Provo knew how to spell "sellout," let alone "loge," beg to keep coaching. "When do I want him to retire?" says Lance Reynolds, one of several longtime Edwards aides who is in good position to mount a campaign to become his replacement. "I hope he never retires."

I became personally aware of what it's like to work with LaVell Edwards during the past year as we collaborated on the manuscript for this book. Hard as this may be to believe, after we had completed the interviewing process, not once did he tell me how or what to write. He didn't tell me who to interview, or what to leave in or take out—*of his own book.* When he gives you a job to do, he gets out of your way and lets you do it. The master delegator, no matter what.

His only request was a self-deprecating tweak: "Make it so I don't sound like a P.E. major from Utah State."

I tried to do that. I also tried to put into words the subtleties and the "feel" of a most complex yet most simple man. It wasn't easy but it was a pleasure just the same. Like Lance Reynolds, I too hope LaVell Edwards never retires. We could do another book.

—LEE BENSON
SANTA BARBARA, CALIFORNIA

CHAPTER ONE

Perceptions

For the record, let me begin by saying that when the position for head football coach at Brigham Young University opened up in January of 1972, if I had thought about it—which I didn't—I probably wouldn't have hired me, either.

My resumé was not even close to impeccable. Rival schools were not beating down my door with offers. I had spent the ten years just passed at BYU, where I was originally hired because of my expertise with an offense—the single wing—that had been scrapped eight years previous along with the head coach who favored it. After that they turned me into a defensive coach, where I thrived personally if not professionally. Which is to say we were not exactly world-beaters. Our win-loss record was stuck in the throes of mediocrity, at best. Of the ten BYU teams I'd been part of, just four had managed winning records, and after the 1971 season we were on something of a skid, having lost fifteen of our last twenty-three games. Add to that the fact that during my eight years of high school coaching, all of them spent as the head coach at Granite High School in Salt Lake City, I never experienced a winning season. It wasn't that we were noncompetitive at Granite, which, to be fair, was the smallest school in the city at the time and consequently at something of a disadvantage, numbers-wise. I was proud of the caliber of my players. I was satisfied that we battled in every game, and typically we'd finish with a record of 3 and 5 or sometimes 4 and 4, and barely miss the playoffs.

Still, add it up and as a high school and

college coach I had experienced four winning records in eighteen seasons. Hardly the stuff of glittering resumés, let alone successful job interviews. Hardly the credentials that promotions are typically made of.

As I said, if I'd thought about it, that might have posed as big a problem for me as it must have posed for those who wondered what on earth BYU was doing when they hired me. But I didn't give it anything but cursory thought.

Thinking very much about the past—no matter what might have happened, good, bad, whatever—is not my nature. When people ask me how I feel when I reflect on, say, winning the national championship, or how I'm affected by what happened the last time we played an opponent, and I answer, "I really don't think about it," well, I really don't think about it. I never have. Probably never will. I'm not saying history isn't a good teacher. I'm not saying we can't learn from reflecting on the past. I'm not saying thinking about the past is bad or unproductive. I'm just saying I'm not very good at it. I don't do it very much. I don't think about where I've been nearly as much as about where I am, and where that might take me.

I do worry. I'm a world-class worrier. I can worry as much as Bill Clinton on a bad day. I once got an ulcer from worrying too much, which may surprise some people. But I don't worry about what's happened, about what's gone on before. I worry about what might happen. I was like that in 1972, and to a large extent, I'm still like that, although I no longer have the ulcer.

Also for the record, I had no grandiose plan in place that gray night in January of 1972 when I said yes and became the eleventh head football coach at BYU. In no way, shape, or form was my head filled with a master scheme that would revolutionize the program, the region, and the game. I had not planned and plotted my entire life with an eye focused on the fateful day when a college program would be mine and I could finally put all my ideas to the test.

COACHING: A FICKLE PROFESSION

The truth was almost completely the opposite. I enjoyed coaching very much, always had, but at the age of forty-one and with nearly two decades already invested in the business, I was very much spooked by the profession's fickle nature. By 1972 I'd seen my share of surefire game plans go awry. At BYU I'd already been a part of two staffs that were disbanded, and each of the head coaches I'd served under, Hal Mitchell and then Tommy Hudspeth, were men with extensive football backgrounds who, in my estimation, went way beyond simply being competent as coaches. They worked as hard as any other coaches I knew, and I tended to think they cared even more. They knew football. They knew the game on both sides of the ball. If they couldn't make it . . . well, it made me understandably nervous when I inherited the chair they'd both sat in.

Hal Mitchell grew up in California and was an All-American lineman at UCLA, where he also coached before coming to BYU. He was a person of outstanding character, and he understood football inside and out. His plan was to resurrect the single-wing offense and since I was probably the only Mormon in the world coaching the single wing, which I ran at Granite, Hal hired me in 1962, his second season at BYU. He would be gone the next year, after his third season. Eight wins and twenty-two losses in three years successfully got rid of the single wing, and Hal, and gave way to Tommy Hudspeth, an outstanding coach in his own right. Tommy had played a little professional football and came from Tulsa, where he had good coaching results. He had tremendous charisma and was an excellent recruiter, and he used those skills to find quick success. In only his second year, the 1965 season, BYU won the WAC championship, the first time in history the school could claim a league football title. Our record that year was just 6–4, but we won all the right games for the league championship; and when that '65 season was followed by an 8–2 record in 1966, with a second-place finish to Arizona State in the WAC, it seemed that Tommy Hudspeth and BYU had a partnership that would last forever.

But it didn't. After three losing seasons in a four-year span from 1968 through 1971, Tommy and BYU parted company, which is when I came in, the only BYU football coach still standing who could remember back as long as a decade.

Having a ringside seat to watch such job insecurity had an impact on me, to say the least. Someone once told me that whenever you had a winning season or did something good, it meant you could probably count on three more seasons before they'd fire you. The experiences of my first two "mentors" had certainly borne that out. As a hedge against an uncertain coaching future, I went to work on my doctorate—in education—while I was a member of Tommy's staff. I reasoned that if and/or when push came to shove, I could remain at BYU as a professor when my coaching days were over. My thinking was that it wasn't a matter of if I'd get fired, it was a matter of when. I had already survived two staff changeovers. Since I was now the chief of staff, it would be impossible to survive the next one.

As the spring of 1972 approached—my first spring practice as a college head coach—the only thing I knew for sure was this: I had three more years.

Having that realistic (some would say fatalistic) insight into my chosen profession would prove to be most helpful to me, as would any of a number of other insights picked up while I was a developing football coach. If it's true that we are nothing more than the sum total of our experiences, my experiences prior to assuming command of the BYU program couldn't, in hindsight, have been much more perfectly suited to preparing me for the task at hand. I'm very much convinced of that. I owe a lot to my preparation and to the people who prepared me. This applies to both negatives and positives. There was no way I could say I went into the job as BYU's head football coach with my eyes closed.

As I said, my experiences working with both Hal Mitchell and Tommy Hudspeth were invaluable in many regards. To this day I regard both as visionary coaches. Hal's strategy to return to the single-wing offense was his attempt to circumvent the college football status quo that kept struggling programs (like BYU) from making inroads into the big time. The status quo basically worked like this: the traditionally powerful schools successfully recruited virtually all of the country's top players, especially at the skill positions, and then they used strong running attacks to roll over schools with teams made up of lesser recruits.

Hal reasoned that employing a radically different offense would make it difficult for other teams to prepare, plus he wouldn't have to rely on recruiting the big, strong running backs who would turn him down anyway.

Since the single wing—which calls for a direct snap from the center to a single running back—had been the offense of choice in the 1930s, Mitchell thought, why couldn't it be just as successful in the 1960s. He'd played at UCLA when the Bruins were one of the last big-name teams to use the single wing. By 1960, I think Princeton was the only major school in the country still running the single wing—and Hal was going to bring it back.

The thing is, he succeeded. It worked; it really did. In 1962, the season I joined Hal Mitchell's staff, our single-wing running back, Eldon Fortie, was practically unstoppable. He carried the ball 199 times that season for 1,149 yards, both school records, and his 5.8 yards per carry was the best average in the conference. All this from a 5-foot-11, 170-pound running back from Salt Lake City who had learned the single wing playing for me at Granite High School.

But if Fortie was difficult to stop, the same wasn't true for the offense as a whole, and the real problem was that you couldn't get much better because you really couldn't recruit to the single wing anymore. Kids weren't familiar with it. They didn't want to play something they didn't know. That '62 team went 4–6 and the '63 team went 2–8. End of experiment.

If Hal's brainstorm had said "wishbone," an option offense about to become the rage of the day, instead of "single wing," his career at BYU might have had a different outcome. As it was he was a victim of his own experiment. But he was on the right track in a way. Hal was kind of a dreamer and I think he saw a lot of things the rest of us didn't. He used to sit in the office and say, "I'll tell you guys, one day BYU is going to be a great football power, a great football school." He liked to tinker and he liked to dream. After he left coaching he went to work for Rawlings Sporting Goods and had a successful career with them, helping to design and invent new equipment.

Tommy Hudspeth also steered away from conventional football. As a recruiter he tried several innovative things. He dispatched me, as his recruiting coordinator, to Chicago to talk a twenty-six-year-old bus driver named Paul Devine into enrolling at BYU. Devine became the first black to come to BYU to play football, although for a variety of reasons he never actually suited up. More black athletes were to follow because of Tommy's vision. Tommy also recruited a number of former U.S. Marines in an attempt to bring maturity, discipline, and a quick physical fix to the program, and it was Tommy who succeeded in freeing his staff from classroom teaching duties, turning us all into full-time coaches. Too, Tommy had a good eye for talent and using it accordingly. When it became obvious that a raw recruit named Virgil Carter had the tools to be something special at quarterback, we went to a passing attack that was quite liberal at the time. Carter's passes were the main ingredient in that first-ever conference championship in 1965 and in the 8–2 record that followed in 1966. But then Virgil's eligibility ran out and the offense returned to a more conventional approach.

Contrary to what some statistical historians might theorize, these coaches, and those who preceded them, were hardly just "going through the paces" at BYU, a supposed football graveyard. Their example, and their ways of thinking, had a lot to do with the success that would come in their wake, a lot more than they probably have ever realized.

But something was missing and that was obvious. Since just after the end of World War II, when Eddie Kimball ended an eight-season run as head coach with a 34–32–8 record, BYU had gone through five head coaches in a little over twenty years, none of the five managing to win more games than he lost. An attitude had simultaneously cropped up that gained steam as the losing trend got longer—an attitude that said Brigham Young University and football were not compatible.

THE MYTHS OF DEFEAT

A number of theories tried to suggest why this was so. The most popular said that football, a violent game, could not peacefully coexist with the atmosphere of a private Christian school, and that the Mormon Church's missionary program, which often interrupted a football player's career with a two-year leave of absence, changed players into pacifists who weren't inclined to hit anybody very hard when they came home, if they were inclined to play football at all.

Those were the beliefs, and every year when BYU had another unsuccessful season, they gained momentum. It was a self-perpetuating kind of thing. We couldn't win because it was a church school; the Mormon Church and football weren't compatible. Recruiting was therefore difficult, at best, and even if we ever did get somebody good, somebody who could play, it was because he was a great member of the Church, not because he wanted to play football at BYU. And if he was that kind of kid, at the appropriate age he'd go on a mission—and then he'd come back to school and never play again.

That was the party line, and it became a staff habit to go over it again and again. I don't know how many staff meetings we sat through that ended with us rehashing the same old reasons why we couldn't win. Invariably the conclusion would be that we couldn't survive here; we couldn't win here. We had all the reasons down pat. The Church connection was only part of the problem. We had a smaller staff than any of the schools we played. Utah and Utah State had eight assistant coaches, and some of the big schools back East had maybe twice that many. (This was in the days when there weren't restrictions on staff size.) We had just six coaches on our staff. And we didn't have a lot of money to recruit players. That was still another thing. We had quite a list. There were just a lot of things we didn't have or couldn't do. And we dwelled on them.

Then I inherited the whole package.

Somewhere along the line I remember the thought occurring to me that, you know, there really isn't anything I can do—at least not immediately—about the fact that I don't have as many assistants as Utah or Utah State, or about not having all the money we needed to adequately recruit. There were a lot of things we didn't have, but there was really nothing I could do about a lot of them. So I decided I wouldn't focus on those things. What good was it to worry about things we couldn't change?

To survive, we had to stop thinking about the negative. We had to change the image we had of ourselves. We had to accept who we were and see ourselves in a positive light.

I could say that I saw this clearly in 1972—as clearly as hindsight would reveal the impact of positive thinking years later. But the truth is, it wasn't something that dawned on me all of a sudden. It was more of an intuitive feeling. Instinctively I just felt that if football and BYU were going to get along, we needed to perceive ourselves in a different way.

Our problem was perception.

And besides, I never did buy into the notion that Mormon kids couldn't play football. For one thing, it didn't jibe with my own experiences. I'd played college football at Utah State, where most of the team was Mormon, and we'd had success. I grew up in Orem and I couldn't remember there being a lot then about Mormon kids not being compatible with football. To me that theory never carried weight. Mormon kids aren't a whole lot different from anybody else. As far as the desire to compete, you don't see any more fierce competitors. Whenever I hear theories that kids who go to church don't make good football players I think of Mel Olson, who played for BYU and then was a part of my first coaching staff. On the field, you couldn't find a more intense, ferocious competitor. But off the field, you couldn't provoke him no matter how hard you tried.

People say things like "football players don't turn the other cheek." Well, in an athletic contest you don't turn the other cheek because it's a game and that's what it's about, to defend, to not back down. I don't want to come off as an authority on the religious aspects of turning the other cheek, but I believe that when it comes to football it simply does not apply. You don't defend out of anger or provocation. Guys aren't trying to kill each other. You might hear that expression, but the players don't honestly want to hurt each other. That's not the object. That's not the game. The game is about people loving to compete. And those people who like to compete with physical contact often love to compete on a football field.

I know that, because I was one of them. When I played I had only one worry: What would I do when I couldn't play anymore? I didn't like playing football—I loved playing football. I loved everything about it: the contact, the competition, the strategy. One of the main reasons I went into coaching was that it let me stay in the game even after I'd stopped playing. Coaching is a way to keep competing. I'm a lot more competitive than a lot of people probably know, and football has always provided a great way for me to compete.

I think the reason football and the Church environment at BYU (any religious environment for that matter) can not only coexist, but thrive, is that once you get past a few commonly held misconceptions the two are quite compatible. While it's true that football is a physical game, it is also a challenging game that is more strategic and tactical than anything else; and in that way it requires real discipline and control if you're going to have any success. Dismissing it as a brutal exercise that gives people an excuse to try to hurt each other misses the point. Quite to the contrary, football does a lot to teach the same things that a Church environment tries to teach. There are a lot of similarities. In coaching, you teach love and you teach togetherness and you teach serving each other and a lot of other things that Christianity itself is also concerned with. There's really a great deal of love developed on a football team, at least on the good ones. The feelings you have for each other, the relationships you develop—and that includes with your opponent—reflect a lot of mutual respect. Competition very often brings out the very best in people.

So I never felt that football and religion couldn't coexist or, by the same token, that you couldn't recruit football players, Mormon or non-Mormon, to BYU. I never felt that was the issue. I thought the issue was more one of commitment, both by the coaching staff and the administration, to really believing in the sport at BYU and supporting it to the extent that it could be successful.

The more I thought about it, the more I came to the same kind of feeling about what was seen as "the missionary problem." Those perceptions about returned missionaries not being able to play just didn't make any sense. Again, I could say it came to me all at once; I could say that as soon as I became head coach I put into operation this preconceived scheme to use the missionary program to help the BYU football team become a national power. That would make a great story. But in truth it usually takes me a while to work things out. And that's what happened with the way we changed our attitudes about missionaries. It was a gradual process.

My first thought was that I just wanted to change the way we looked at missionaries. At the time, the relationship between the football program and the missionary program was somewhat adversarial. For one thing, any player who went on a mission had to earn his scholarship back when he returned. For another, we encouraged players to finish their four years of eligibility and then go on their missions. They wouldn't go when they were nineteen—the year they were first eligible—but they'd wait until they were twenty-two or twenty-three.

A couple of things happened to affect my thinking. One, my own boys started to grow up, and I got to thinking, I don't know if I want someone to try to talk John and Jim out of going on a mission when they are of age. Another thing was that President Spencer W. Kimball became the prophet about that time and he placed a greater emphasis on kids going on missions.

I made up my mind I wasn't going to fight the system anymore, and I wasn't going to look at it as a negative. I wasn't going to talk anyone out of going when he wanted to go, and I was going to give missionaries their scholarships when they came back, no questions asked.

To that end, I started to write to the missionaries while they were gone. I'd tell them we were supportive of what they were doing and that there would be a scholarship for them when they got back.

I wanted to create an environment for the missionaries that would help them get back into football when they returned, not help drive them away. If a missionary wasn't ready to play when he got back—and that was the case most of the time—he could redshirt and still keep his scholarship. When he was ready, he could play again. There were no hard and fast rules, but that was the general pattern.

Again, the whole thing was about us changing our perception: from "missionaries can't play" to "missionaries can play." It was no more complicated than that. What we found was that the only guys who didn't play when they came back were the same guys who wouldn't have played even if they'd stayed. The missions didn't do it.

What was ironic was that after returned missionaries became a big part of our personnel picture, many people argued that was the main reason we won. Now we had all these old guys who were stronger and more experienced and physically mature, and that gave us an advantage. The same people who earlier had felt sorry for us because of the missionary program were now saying the missionary program was giving us an unfair advantage. We went from one extreme to the other. Which was fine by me.

One perception we had of ourselves in 1972 that I thought *was* correct was the notion that we couldn't win by playing conventional football. Hal Mitchell was right. We really did have to do something different. At every level of football you've got your haves and your have-nots, and if you happen to be a have-not you'd better do something creative. At that time BYU was a have-not.

That's the reason we started to throw the football. It was a different approach. It was risky, no question. But it was a way out of the have-nots, if there was a way. One of the first coaches I hired—in addition to those who stayed on from Tommy's staff—was Dewey Warren, a former quarterback at Tennessee who knew a lot about throwing the football. Or, as he put it, "thowing" the football. Then we got lucky our first year and, although we hadn't yet gone to the passing game, we went 7 and 4 and tied for second place in the league. That created a lot more interest in us than we'd had in a while. We got a few people's attention. They were wondering what we were up to.

To tell the truth, we were wondering the same thing. That first year was a feeling-out period as much as anything. As I said, I knew I wanted to throw the ball more. That was always in the back of my mind. But in

1972 we had an outstanding senior running back named Pete Van Valkenburg. Pete wound up leading the country in rushing while carrying the new staff on his back.

Starting with a winning season was invaluable. The success we had that first year helped in many ways, not the least of which was allowing us to expand the size of our coaching staff. I had just the six assistant coaches when I began, the same as Tommy before me and Hal before him. On offense, that first staff was made up of Dave Kragthorpe, J. D. Helm, Mel Olson, and Dewey Warren. Defensively there were two coaches, Dick Felt and Jim Criner. For years, Dick Felt and I had made up the defensive staff, and when I became head coach I hired Jim Criner to take my old position.

As I've said, our staff size was at least two coaches fewer than most of the other schools in the region. Over time, I was hoping to do something about that. When Jim Criner accepted an offer to join the staff at UCLA at the end of the season, that gave us an opening. I decided to see just how much we could capitalize on the good first year we'd just had, so I sat down and wrote a lengthy letter to the athletic director and the dean of the college of physical education. I explained that we needed to replace one coach, and since I knew of two LDS coaches, Fred Whittingham and Tom Ramage, who were both outstanding and knowledgeable and interested in working at BYU, and since we were understaffed compared to such places as Utah and Utah State—well, why not go ahead and hire both of them. To my delight the administration said okay, and we were able to add Tom Ramage and Fred Whittingham to the defense, giving BYU a three-man defensive staff for the first time ever.

My mindset was still very much focused on sheer survival going into our second year, but there were a lot of things I was feeling positive about. We'd started off on a good note. We had an expanded staff. And, most important, our self-image was changing—something I instinctively knew was the key to our survival. If we didn't view ourselves as legitimate, why would anyone else? If we didn't, would our recruits? our fans? our opponents? I just knew that was essential and it had to continue.

We needed to perceive BYU as a university where football wasn't just something that filled the gap between the start of school and the start of basketball season. We needed to ignore the negatives we couldn't do anything about, and those that we could do something about we needed to turn into positives. Yes, we had our peculiarities; we had things that were unique to us; and some of them presented certain challenges. But when you think about it, doesn't every school? Doesn't every situation?

Fortunately, our self-image improved rather rapidly during those first few years. We were lucky in a lot of ways. The new approach to handling missionaries turned out to be a plus. The administration proved to be as committed to the program as we coaches were. And most of all, the decision to go to a passing game paid dividends beyond any we had imagined, both on the field and in recruiting. All those things made it easier for us to turn around the way we thought of ourselves.

The perceptions others had of BYU also started to change. In coaching, you know you're doing something right when coaches from other schools visit your spring practices. For years, we'd spread out around the country as BYU coaches, looking at how the successful schools ran their programs, trying to learn something from them to take back home. We were always the ones that visited them. We were the ones with all the frequent-flyer miles.

Now there was some reciprocation going on. At first we weren't quite sure how we should act. I remember the first time we got a request from some Michigan coaches who wanted to visit Provo and spend a few days watching our practices. We wondered if we should send a car to the airport to pick them up.

Changing the way we looked at ourselves was a gradual process and it required effort, but as we succeeded in changing the perception we had of ourselves, it was obvious that the perception of others changed too. When we stopped looking at BYU as a private church school that couldn't successfully coexist with major college football, a lot of other people stopped looking at us that way, too.

"Sanky"

*Donald L. Dixon,
LaVell's first coach*

Donald L. "Sanky" Dixon opens his mailbox and inside finds a letter from one of the boys he coached . . . almost a half-century ago.

Some things only get better with age. Like this. Sanky Dixon and the letter writer, LaVell Edwards, got acquainted on the football field at Lincoln High School before Milton Berle was a TV star; and that was just the start of it. Now Sanky isn't a coach anymore. He's in his late 80s—"fast closing in on 100," he says. And LaVell isn't a player anymore. He's coaching up the road at BYU. And yet they're as close as they've ever been, or maybe closer. If they're not talking on the phone they're either visiting in person or they're trading letters.

Sanky lives in room 327 at The Seville, a modern retirement center in Orem, Utah, about ten miles from the BYU campus and maybe five miles from where he once coached. He would be the first to tell you that Orem has changed. Most of the orchards are gone now, replaced by car washes, Eat-a-Burgers, Circle Ks, and street after street of houses. There must be ten thousand times as much asphalt now as there used to be.

But when Sanky squints his eyes he can easily see Orem's old Lincoln High, named after the president. The school buildings were torn down long ago, but not in his mind. In the fall especially, the parking lot outside his window turns back into fruit trees, and the grainy black-and-white photograph on the coffee table in front of him turns back into living color.

The picture is of Sanky, dressed in a suit and a tie and a hat, sitting on top of his players' shoulders as they carry him off the football field. Lincoln High has just won the 1948 state championship. The player carrying Sanky's right ankle, wearing a huge grin, is LaVell Edwards. LaVell was a linebacker on defense, a center on offense, and Sanky's all-around "coach on the field."

"I had LaVell call signals for me," Sanky says. "He really understood the game. And man, he loved it."

Loved his coach, too.

"He's always kept in touch," Sanky says, waving today's mail for proof. There is a letter on BYU football stationery. The note inside is short. It closes with:

> I do love you very much and I'm so
> proud to have played for Sanky Dixon.
> Take care.
> Love you,
> LaVell

"He always ends with 'I love you' or something like that," Sanky says. "And he's always got some kind of joke going. The other day he sent me an application form for the head job at BYU. He said he'd submitted my name. He said, 'He can't see very well, he can't hear very well, and he has to use a cane. But he sure has a lot of experience.'"

Sanky laughs. There have been a lot of laughs over the years. The good old days, then and now.

He coached LaVell and four of his brothers at Lincoln High. "They were tough kids," Sanky says. "They put everything into it when they played. Football was a big thing back then in this area, and you didn't have to worry about the kids training or anything like that. They'd practice and then they'd walk home and do their chores. There were just a lot of good kids who wanted to play football."

"All of them were defensive players," he says, speaking specifically of the Edwards boys again.

Why is that? he is asked.

"Oh, I don't know, I guess because they liked to hit," he says. And then the best coach in the history of Lincoln High School gets a big smile on his face. "And I don't think they were very fast."

CHAPTER TWO

Roots

It would be hard to understate the impact my first football coach had on me.

I was eight years old when we met. I was watching my older brothers practice at the old Lincoln High School in Orem, Utah. It was my routine that every day in the fall after elementary school was over, I'd walk across the street to the high school and watch football practice before walking on home to the farm. I had a double motive. One was that I loved the sights and sounds of football practice, and I loved to watch my brothers play. The other was that I always hoped that maybe, one day, I'd get home and the cows would be milked.

That never happened, but you had to like my persistence. Every day on my way home, like clockwork, I'd watch Lincoln High's football practice.

So it was that I came to realize that even if he did have a team to coach practically all by himself (he had one assistant, the basketball coach), Sanky Dixon wasn't the kind of person not to notice a little kid.

He made me his water boy.

Donald L. "Sanky" Dixon, the head football coach at Lincoln High School for what seemed like forever, was held in high esteem among the farmers and fruit growers of Orem, Utah. He was an accomplished athlete himself. He had a brother named Buck who coached tennis and golf at BYU, and together they won about every tennis title you could win in the West, and several national honors as well. Sanky's football teams at Lincoln High played hard, played fair, and had great success. He was a very popular coach with his players, with their parents, with the entire town. He could have run for mayor and won—but why would he want to do that when he had such a gift for making football fun and competitive at the same time? I idolized him.

He was neither a complicated man nor a complicated coach. He used the single-wing offense and never departed from it. He had five or six basic plays, and he was as loyal to those plays as they were to the win-loss record of his Lincoln High Tigers. A spy would have died of boredom watching our practices. There was absolutely no secret to what we were going to do.

Every day in practice we would go over the same things, time and time again, and every Friday on game day we would run those same plays. The day before the state championship game, which we played in both my junior year (lost) and senior year (won), I remember going over the basics of blocking and tackling, of starts, stances, and take-offs.

At Lincoln High we never strayed from our routine. Sanky was a stickler for fundamentals. Sometimes as players we'd try to get to him—the way players will do. We'd say something like, "How do we block on a 25, Coach?" knowing full well how we were supposed to block on a 25 since we'd been practicing the play for what seemed like most of our lives. And Sanky wouldn't miss a beat. He'd say, "Well, let's get the play-book and take a look," and without fail he'd send the manager to find his playbook, which consisted of about three old, worn pages held together by a ring. Then he'd go over all the options. For the 25 you could use a 6–2 defense, or a 5–3, or a 7–diamond—and that was it, the sum total of the defenses Sanky had us use.

I played center and linebacker for Sanky Dixon, the same positions all my brothers played before me. I had a real passion, I guess you could say, for defense. I always enjoyed the contact. As for playing center in the old single wing, it was not a position for the weak of heart. The offense called for the center to hike the ball directly to the ball carrier—and ball carriers were as temperamental then as they are now. If we were running a 29, say, then they wanted the ball right here, and if it was a 25 they wanted it right there. That's where they needed it so they could hit the hole properly, and if the ball wasn't right where it was supposed to be, well, you know who the backs—and the coaches—would yell at. The center, of course. Which was me. And all the time you've got some guy positioned across from you just waiting for you to hike the ball so he can knock your head off. But you're not looking at him, because you're looking backwards through your legs. I don't know why my brothers started playing center for Sanky, but by the time I came around he simply expected me to do the same—so I did.

With practice you could get good at it. Like I said, at Lincoln High we did not dodge working on fundamentals, or repetitively working on the same plays. We did have one play where three running backs would line up at various positions in the backfield, with none of them directly behind the center. When you got down and looked through your legs, nobody would be there. Then they'd start barking out signals, and all of a sudden the wingback would come running and you had to snap the ball to him on the dead run. The timing had to be perfect. It was our trick play. We practiced that play for three years . . . and never did use it.

Sanky's penchant for detail and repetition had a major impact on me, an impact that would mold the way I would later coach. At Lincoln High I knew, and so did everyone else, that we had no lock on what we were doing. Our single wing wasn't any different from anyone else's single wing. It wasn't that difficult to figure out. All it ever came down to was a basic matter of execution. The question was always whether we could execute our offense better than our opponents could execute their defense. It was that simple.

During my years at BYU it's essentially been the same thing. Our basic pass routes, for instance, haven't changed for twenty years. We'll add to them and make some modifications, of course, but basically our offense is the same as it's always been. It's never been that difficult to figure out, either.

Every spring and every fall we start with the basic elements of blocking and tackling and execution, of running the same route every

time, of doing it all with as much precision as possible. I think all successful football teams have that approach to the fundamentals. Look at
Notre Dame. They get great athletes, it's true, but they're very basic in
what they do—and they do it very well. That's why I think Lou Holtz is
an excellent football coach. He emphasizes the basics. And when you
play someone like that, you realize that football isn't just lining up and
overpowering people. It's not just a game of who wants it more. The
fine points of blocking and tackling and reading coverages and all the
rest of it—that's what really matters. Who does it better? Who executes?
That's the game. Thanks to Sanky Dixon, I was exposed to that early
on.

Sanky took a lot of personal interest in his players, and I was no
exception. He used to talk to me about going on to college. He'd tell me
that I had enough ability to play on that level if I wanted to, and he'd
stress the value of a college education. That meant a lot to me. He built
me up. He really cared about me as a person.

He was a disciplinarian to a point, but not to the point where you
were all that aware of it. Mainly he'd get discipline from you because
you respected him so much you didn't want to let him down. I will
never forget the day I let him down the most. It was when I was a
sophomore and I was getting kind of cocky because I was playing football and basketball and people were starting to notice who I was. One
day we were fooling around with a wet towel in the locker room, and I
picked it up and threw it and it hit Sanky in the side of the face. He
called me into his office and said, "You may be a good athlete, you may
come from a fine family, and you may have a lot of friends. But, you
know, that does not give you license to be a jerk."

That had a tremendous impact on me. I've long since forgotten
what precipitated that towel incident, but I'll never forget what Sanky
Dixon said to me, or the embarrassment I felt. I didn't want to do anything like that ever again. I think that incident's had a lot to do with the
way I deal with things today. I know a lot of times I've called kids in and
given them the same speech Sanky gave me, almost verbatim. More
often than not, it's worked.

DAD, MOM, AND WHY I'M THE WAY I AM

In a lot of ways, Sanky was like my father. Both tended to show you rather than tell you. Their examples exceeded their words. As my father wrote at the conclusion of his personal history, which he completed not long before he died, "I have never spent time preaching to my family, but I have tried to live like I would want them to live." My mother was like that, too.

They died within three weeks of each other in 1989, my mother, Addie May Gurr Edwards, who was ninety-two, and my father, Philo Taylor Edwards, who was ninety. After seventy-two years of marriage, no one was surprised when they went out together.

I was the eighth of the fourteen children they raised, counting a cousin who lived with us and whom I always thought of as a sister. I was a middle child—No. 8 in a lineup that included seven boys and seven girls. I guess you could say I started the second half.

My father did a variety of jobs throughout his life, but my youth coincided mostly with the days he spent farming in Orem. I was born on October 11, 1930, in my grandmother's house in Provo, not far from the BYU campus. The Great Depression was just warming up, to be followed by World War II, and my childhood was spent amid what some might call, in the politically correct '90s, economic adversity.

We didn't have many luxuries, and as a young person I can never remember having a nickel of my own. But still, I never thought of us as being poor. Everything was relative, of course, and not a lot of other people had a lot back then either, but I credit my parents for the way they didn't draw attention to what we might be lacking.

Some people like to talk about being poor; they like to talk about never having had anything. They almost wear it like a badge. But I never knew we didn't have a lot. I never felt that we were poor or that we were less important than anyone else.

My mother generated that kind of thinking. She had a positive outlook throughout her life that spilled over onto her family. She had a way of keeping everything going smoothly and keeping our emotions from running too high or too low. I remember picking up the evening paper one night at home and reading that I'd been named to the all-state football team. I showed my mother. "That's nice," she said. "You should be very grateful for that. By the way, are the cows milked?"

She maintained that kind of perspective all her life. Many years later, on January 2, 1985, the day the BYU football team her son was coaching was declared the national champion by both the AP and UPI polls, she noted the news in her diary. This is what she wrote: "Good news. BYU is number one in the nation." And then, without even starting a new paragraph: "Such wonderful news from Don and Mary. They are going on a mission."

My father had an incredible range and capacity for work. Born to homesteader parents in a small place that doesn't exist anymore (Buckhorn Flats in southern Utah), he didn't go any further than the eighth grade. And yet I saw him on any number of occasions counsel Church leaders, community leaders, doctors, and college professors who came to him for help and advice. He was the stake president in the Orem area for a number of years, and a bishop before that. He was also president of the school board. He wore a lot of hats. To make a living, he hauled fruit and coal and he was a dairy farmer and a fruit farmer. Later, he went into land development.

He never was a football coach, but I think he would have made a terrific one. You're always putting out fires as a coach, and that's the way it was with just about everything he was involved in—especially the farm. He was a great one for getting the job done, without making a lot of commotion about it. He almost never made speeches, in any of his responsibilities. He'd watch a lot, and when he made changes he'd make them subtly.

I'm sure that a lot of the style I have as a football coach—and in other areas of leadership—goes back to the way my dad did things.

Dad would get after you if you didn't do something he'd asked, but he wouldn't get after you if you'd tried and hadn't done it right. He'd let you work at it until you got it. He wouldn't just take over. To me, that's always been a very important principle, because that's how people are allowed to develop. If you're in charge and something's happening that will create a problem, then of course you have to step in and help out the situation; but a lot of times those doing the work are going to figure it out themselves, and if you allow them that freedom, they'll grow because of the experience. I know that was the case for me.

There was no mistaking the importance of the family during my upbringing—even though, again, little was said about it. We'd always sit down and have breakfast together and then do the same at dinner, and we always knelt to pray before we ate. Thinking back on it, mealtime was really quite a sight. We had a big, oblong table with a bench next to the wall and chairs that went around the other sides. The bench held four, maybe five, kids; that's where the younger ones sat. As you got older you got to move out to one of the chairs.

There was a definite hierarchy in our family, although little was said about that, either. As you got older you just naturally moved on to other things—where you sat at the table, beds, chores, and so on. You just knew your place. You instinctively knew your role. It was an atmosphere that was conducive to getting along. There was always somebody else to think about.

We used to fight with each other, but if we ever fought with anybody else we stuck together in it. I guess large families inspire that kind of loyalty. For years I've joked that the reason BYU keeps me around as football coach is that my family buys so many season tickets. I've wondered how many of them would buy season tickets if I weren't the head coach. Some of them really like football, of course, and would go to the games no matter who was coaching. But there are some who really like football because their brother is the coach. There's a lot of loyalty in our family.

When Dad was the stake president, it was common for general authorities from the Church to come to the house for dinner during stake conferences. One enduring memory of those visits is that we didn't have to act any differently when they were there than when they weren't. I've thought about that a lot as I've grown older. There was never any contradiction between what my father did in public and what he did at home. I think some people act different in public, and I think some people behave differently when someone important comes around. My dad wasn't like that with himself or with his family.

He had a way of emphasizing things that were important and not worrying about the rest. An example of that was the night I drove our 1948 Oldsmobile into the yard with the left front end smashed in. This wasn't just any old car. This was the first car the Edwards family ever owned—and at the time of the crash we'd owned it for approximately two weeks.

After the war things had begun to turn around for us economically. We'd remodeled the house and bought that car, which came at the end of a long line of trucks. It was a beautiful new car. I'd taken it on a date and was coming back from Pleasant Grove in a rainstorm when we suddenly came upon some railroad tracks. I jammed on the brakes, and the car went into a spin that didn't stop until we ran into the railroad crossing sign.

It wasn't a major accident but, still, I was not feeling real good about life as I drove into the yard and got out of my father's Oldsmobile. My dad took one look and said, "Anybody get hurt?" I told him no and then I told him how it happened and that was it. Accidents happen; that was his attitude. His one and only real concern was, "Anybody get hurt?"

My dad had a great ability to keep me in line. When he either knew, or guessed, that I wasn't doing the things I ought to be doing, he'd call me in and say, "LaVell, you know a lot of people have problems, but I know one thing. I know I will never have to worry about you." Then he'd return to what he was doing and I'd mumble something like "That's right, Dad." I'd walk away with a guilty conscience and vow to never do anything wrong again. I used to wish he'd get mad at me and really tell me off; then I could get mad back and take off and do what I wanted. That way I could make it his fault. But it never happened.

Although he was completely supportive of athletics, my father never really watched me—or any of my brothers—play ball. Our mother came to our games once in a while after my older sister Melba talked her into coming. But what we did on the football field or the basketball court was never treated like it was the center of the universe. Nor were we ever forced into doing anything, including football. It wasn't that there weren't expectations in our family. To the contrary, there was a strong undercurrent of expectation. It was expected you'd get up and go to church, for instance. Staying in bed was not an option. It was expected you'd live a Christian life. It was expected you'd make a success of yourself. But charting out your own life was your own business. It was fine if my brothers and I wanted to play football, but that didn't mean somebody else would do our chores, or that football would get any more attention than a lot of other things.

COLLEGE AWAY FROM THE COWS

I can't ever remember my parents talking to me about going to college. But they didn't talk to me about not going to college, either. They inspired in all of us a good deal of personal pride and independence. They let us feel that we were free to make our own choices.

Somehow they made us all feel like we were each their individual favorite. I know I always felt that way growing up. It wasn't until later on, when we compared notes as adult brothers and sisters, that it came out that we all felt that way. We all thought we were our parents' favorite. All fourteen of us.

They didn't have any Dr. Spock books to help them, or sessions with child psychologists, but our parents had that innate ability to make their kids feel good about themselves.

I was the first in the family to go to college, and football helped pay the way. I suppose everyone, and this included me, assumed that I would go to BYU—the campus was practically next door to the farm. Two BYU coaches, Eddie Kimball and Wayne Soffe, came out one night and took my parents and me to dinner. That was the extent of their recruiting, and it was enough. I was all set to go to BYU.

But then one day in the summer I was out working on the farm and one of my sisters came out to tell me there were a couple of coaches from Utah State waiting at the house to see me. The coaches were Tuff Linford and Paul Marsden, and after we visited for a while they talked me into at least coming up to Logan for a visit. A few days later I drove to Utah State and reported to the football office. It wasn't an over-whelmingly warm reception. They acted like they weren't sure who I was. Eventually they called over to the Sigma Chi house and found a football player, who took me and a friend of mine from California—who was also interested in Utah State—around a little bit. We went to a movie that night and the guy who took us lit up a cigarette, which kind of blew me away. We stayed at the Sigma Chi house, and the next morning I talked to Dick Romney, the head coach, for a few minutes and that was that, the sum total of my recruiting by Utah State.

Then I drove home and with all the casualness of an eighteen-year-old—and believe me, knowing firsthand the flippancy of a teenager's decision-making process has come back to haunt me as a coach—I decided to go to . . . Utah State.

Don't ask me why. In reality, there was no overwhelming reason why I chose the Aggies over BYU. I've joked over the years that the main reason I chose to go away to college was to get away from milking those two cows at home. But you know, the truth is, that had as much to do with it as anything. The entire time I was at Utah State, I never had to milk those cows.

I knew I wanted to be a coach—I'd known ever since I watched Sanky Dixon's practices through the fence when I was eight years old—and I majored in P.E. from the start. I wasn't a particularly serious student, but I tended to become serious when it was necessary and I actually got better grades in college than I did in high school.

Times were different then. You just planned on going to college for four years and getting your degree, which is what I did. Nothing else entered my mind. Back then you didn't change majors too much, or drop classes, or take off for a semester to go motorcycling through the Alps. Redshirting was a thing of the future. There are so many more options now that it's just unreal. In 1949 you went to college for four years and got your degree.

Although I'd been recruited by Dick Romney, the legendary coach who had been at Utah State longer than I'd been alive (his first season was 1919), he stepped down just as I began my sophomore year. His replacement was George Melinkovich, a man I liked and respected a great deal. George was raised in Tooele, Utah, and then played running back at Notre Dame for Knute Rockne. After college he was an outstanding high school coach in New Jersey, which is what he was doing when Utah State hired him.

For a variety of reasons, I actually ended up staying at Utah State longer than George did. After my sophomore and junior seasons he was replaced by John Roning. As it turned out, I wound up having three head coaches in my four seasons as a college football player. Even at that early date I'd gained personal insight into just how tenuous the coaching profession can be.

Coach John Roning had a big impact on me. He was extremely well organized. He knew just what was going on and when and why and by whom. It was like clockwork with John. Like Sanky Dixon, he spent a lot of time on technique. We weren't helter-skelter at all. We were a well-organized, well-disciplined football team. John was a great leader, he was very good-looking, he dressed well, and he carried himself well. He had a tremendous influence on me.

John came to Utah State from Minnesota, where they played the single wing, the same offense I'd grown up with at Lincoln High School. For some reason, that offense and LaVell Edwards always seemed to be running into each other. It would be an understatement to say the single wing was good to me. We won a state championship with it at Lincoln High, and it was my experience with the single wing that got me to BYU in the first place.

During my first three seasons at Utah State we ran our offense out of the T-formation, but we switched to the single wing my last year. John later moved on to coach at the University of Denver, and eventually he became the commissioner of the Big Sky Conference and lived in Boise. Wherever he went I continued to correspond with him. When I was a high school coach starting out at Granite High I would regularly send him information about what we were doing and ask for his assessments. The single-wing offense we ran at Granite was straight out of John Roning's Utah State playbook.

I was fortunate to associate with a long line of excellent coaches who wound up being my mentors as well. All of them helped me develop in what would prove to be my life's work.

ARMY COACH

I thought I would have to take a break from football when I left Utah State and entered an institution that was waiting for me with open arms—the United States Army. I had been in ROTC in college and a full-time, two-year commitment awaited me when I got out. I was commissioned as a second lieutenant and was assigned to Fort Lee, Virginia.

But even though I was all set for regular army life, ready to do whatever they wanted me to do, football came to the rescue. One of the first people I ran into at Fort Lee was Jim Garrett, a teammate from Utah State. He was playing on the post team, and he said there were a lot worse things to do as a soldier than play football. He said he'd talk to the captain in charge of the team about me playing. The next thing I knew, I was playing football for Fort Lee. I guess you could say I was a professional football player. I was getting paid, and I was playing football.

Eventually the army assigned me to what they said was my specialty—food service—and after the football season at Fort Lee I was transferred to Fort Mead, Maryland, where I suspected my football days were finally over. It was at Fort Mead that I found myself in a most uncomfortable teaching situation. Since I was an officer, I was assigned to teach food service to the enlisted men. My classes consisted of small groups of career military men, most of them sergeants and corporals who were much older and more experienced than I was. In the army you get more stripes as you serve more years, and some of these guys in my class had stripes down their entire arms. But since I was a second lieutenant I was supposed to teach them—even though I knew absolutely nothing about the subject.

I'd resigned myself to my fate when, once again, football bailed me out. The post commander heard I'd played football at Fort Lee and that I wanted to be a football coach. He asked me if I'd consider transferring my assignment so I could coach the post team. In the morning I would be assigned to chauffeur a captain around, and in the afternoon I'd coach the base football team. As job offers go, they don't get much better than this one. I told the commander that Fort Mead had a new coach.

My first coaching venture also taught me not to count on anything in coaching, such as longevity. We won our first three games. My lifetime coaching record was 1,000. I was undefeated. I was feeling pretty smug. Then we lost our fourth game and I was sent to the Orient.

The conflict in Korea had a lot to do with that assignment, of course, although I've joked ever since that you talk about tough alumni—well, they don't get any tougher than the army. I lost one game and they shipped me overseas.

The army assigned me to Kokura in southern Japan where I was the post food officer in an R&R center. The troops stationed in Korea—by this time the shooting had stopped but U.S. soldiers were still being sent there—would come to Kokura and a number of other places like it in Japan for furloughs. We'd get calls at all hours of the day or night that troops were coming in and we'd get busy frying a bunch of steaks. The soldiers would come in, have a steak dinner and a place to stay, and then they could come and go as they wanted for seven days or so. Then we'd cook them another steak and send them back to Korea. I might have been sent to Korea myself, but by this time I was having problems with my hip, the result of a tobogganing accident I'd been in my last winter in college.

We'd been in the mountains above Logan, and my feet were sticking out to the side of the toboggan when we crashed. I twisted my hip and was lucky I didn't do more damage than that. The Army doctors examined me and said that because of that bad hip I didn't have to go to Korea if I didn't want to. I said I'd just as soon not and they sent me to Japan.

I worked for a time in food service. Then the post commander called me in and said the equipment officer was leaving—since they didn't have anybody to replace him, would I do it? I said yes and I became the post equipment officer. The outgoing major handed me a clipboard and said, "Here, sign this." So I did and was in charge for the next seven or eight months before I got my papers to go home.

When they replaced me with another major, he wanted to see that everything was in order and therefore did a careful inventory. It turned out that a few things were missing from the original manifest, including a safe and some other things. Of course, they looked at me because I'd originally signed for them. I had no idea what was or wasn't there. Sure, my name was at the bottom of the manifest, but I'd done no inventory when I took over. They checked out my story and told me not to worry about it.

So I went home, and a little later I got a bill from the Army for six hundred thirty dollars. They said I was liable for what was missing. I wrote back, explaining that there had been a full investigation and I had been cleared. I never did hear back from them. For all I know I probably owe the government six billion dollars by now, with interest. But I did learn a lesson about being careful what you sign for.

LESSONS CUT FROM GRANITE

I returned to Utah State and joined John Roning's coaching staff. John had made room for me as a graduate assistant, even though they didn't call it that at the time. I was going to work on my master's degree and help out with the football team.

That was the plan, at any rate. But before fall camp even got underway the plan changed. One day in late August I walked into the athletic department offices and ran into Cec Baker, the longtime basketball coach at Utah State. Cec had just gotten off the telephone with his brother-in-law, Lorenzo Hatch, who was the principal at Granite High School in Salt Lake City. Mr. Hatch had asked Cec if he knew of anybody who might be interested in coaching the football team at Granite. Meaning, right away. The coach they'd hired the past spring, Al Mercer, who had previously been at Cyprus High School, had suddenly decided to move to California. They'd offered the job to Russ Magleby, a counselor at the school and a member of the coaching staff, but he'd turned it down. School was starting in a couple of days, as was the football sea-son, and Granite didn't have a football coach.

Cec told his brother-in-law he'd look around. He didn't have to look far. He turned around and ran into me, almost literally. Things hap-pened that fast.

We got back on the phone and Mr. Hatch asked me to drive down to Salt Lake the next morning with a copy of my transcript. I met with him in the morning. By two o'clock that afternoon I was a high school head coach. No sooner had we shaken hands on a contract that would pay me $3,180 for the school year plus an extra $300 for coaching than the principal said, "Follow me." Together we walked out to the football field—there was the Granite High football team, sitting in full uniform ready to practice. All they needed was a coach.

I learned a lot as a high school coach, and some of the lessons were tough ones. We actually won our first two games; *Deseret News* featured an article about LaVell Edwards resurrecting Granite High football, which had struggled the past few seasons. I thought this coaching busi-ness was going to be easy. Counting my military record, I already had a 5–1 start.

But then, in the third game of the season, reality hit. We were sched-uled to play South High School, which had been picked to finish even lower in the league than Granite. They'd played only one game and had barely beaten Bear River (I think the score was six to nothing). We had seen a picture in one of the newspapers of the South quarterback, a left-handed kid identified as Johnny Day. That was the sum total of the scouting report I gave my team about South. I said to my players, "I don't know much about them except they have this left-hander named Day who is their quarterback."

So we went to South on Friday. On the first play of the game their quarterback dropped back and threw a bullet of a pass right down the middle—right-handed. A little halfback caught the ball and ran for a touchdown. I thought to myself, I could have sworn their quarterback was supposed to be left-handed.

That was just the beginning of the surprises. South ended up beating us 28–0; it wasn't until late in the third quarter that we even got a first down. By that point I was honestly beginning to wonder if we'd ever get one. That little halfback was Lew Duffin, who went on to play at Utah. He also won state that year in the 100-yard dash. The right-handed quarterback was a kid named Frank Christensen, the son of the former Utah All-American of the same name. There was no left-handed quarterback named Day. South went on to win the state championship that season, and I'd had my first lesson in not believing everything you hear or read or see predicted.

That loss was hard for me. I've had plenty of defeats since, but line them all up and ask me which one put me down and kept me there, like a choke hold, and that's the one. It's the worst I ever felt as a football coach. I was devastated. The Utah State Fair was that weekend, and I remember walking around the fairgrounds in a daze. My expectations had been that we'd be pretty good that year, and then we almost hadn't made a first down.

It would be impossible for me to accurately calculate just how much I learned during those eight years at Granite High. But it was plenty. A lot of it came from watching high school coaches who were very good at what they did. If it's true that you learn more from defeat than victory, then this was a very educational time in my life.

One of the most memorable coaches I ever faced was a man named John Vranes, who coached at West High School in Salt Lake City. John was one of those very tough, no-nonsense football coaches. One of our games against him had a particularly great impact on me. It was my second or third year at Granite and we were playing at Granite's field. It was late in the season and had been storming. The field was a quagmire, especially in the middle, which was practically unplayable because of all the mud. Before the game I asked the referee if we could have an agreement that on fourth downs we'd move the ball out of the middle of the field to the drier grass toward the sidelines—so the center and punter would have a reasonable chance. I suppose I was worried we might be punting a lot.

The referee brought John over and he agreed. He just said, "That's fine," very no-nonsense, and that was that. The game proceeded to late in the fourth quarter, and, as fate would have it, we were protecting a two-point lead when we came to fourth down deep in our own territory. We'd just been stopped cold by the West defense on our third-down play, and the West fans were really getting into it as the referee spotted the ball in the middle of the field, right where the mud was at its deepest.

I yelled out to the referee and said, "That's not right! We agreed not to spot the ball there." He said he'd check with John Vranes. He went over to the West sideline, talked to John for a moment, then came back out and moved the ball to dry ground. We got off a clean snap and a good punt and ended up winning the ball game.

After the game I started to walk across the field to shake hands with John. I remember him approaching me with that tough walk and a grim look on his face. Here I was a young coach facing this old veteran, and I couldn't help but wonder, What's going to happen now? How's he going to react? How upset is he going to be with me?

He stuck his hand out and said, "Congratulations. You're going to be a very fine football coach," and walked on in to the visitors' locker room.

That really impressed me. Here the guy had just lost a tough game. He could have complained about moving the ball. He could have told the referee to leave the ball where it was, in the mud, and the referee would have done what John Vranes told him to do. He could have ignored me and just walked off the field and not shaken my hand. But he didn't. He went by what he'd agreed to, even when it hurt to do it, and he didn't cry about it afterward.

There have been a lot of people like John Vranes in my life, who have impacted me in a variety of ways. For the most part it's been the little things that have caught my attention. When I see someone handling a difficult or challenging situation in a good way, I find myself thinking about it and determining to act like that myself. Many of those people who have had the greatest impact on my coaching, as well as other aspects of my life, couldn't have even realized it at the time. But their influence was real, and I'll forever be grateful for it.

Ann Edwards Cannon

John Edwards

Jim Edwards

Home Improvement

Jimmy Edwards froze out of instinct when he saw his third-grade teacher coming toward him. He wasn't sure what he'd done wrong, only that he was about to find out.

Then, a reprieve.

"Your father's outside," his teacher told him. "He wants to see you."

Jimmy walked out of the classroom and saw his dad standing in the hall. His dad took him outside, into the schoolyard, handed him a root beer and said, "I got the job!"

"I'll never forget that day. He dropped everything and came over to tell me," says Jimmy Edwards, now a grown-up, card-carrying attorney who goes by Jim. "I could take you right now and show you the spot on the playground where we were standing when he told me."

LaVell Edwards, Jimmy's father, had been sitting at his desk in the football office that January morning in 1972 when the university president, Dallin H. Oaks, called with the news that they'd like him to be BYU's newest head football coach. He did not put down the phone and immediately alert the media.

He alerted Jimmy.

They'd talked about it for a couple of weeks as BYU went through the process of replacing the outgoing coach, Tommy Hudspeth. Jimmy was a huge fan of the team whose staff his dad had joined a decade earlier, in September of 1962, the month he was born. He'd grown up with the Cougars. During the fall of 1972, he had walked over to the football field almost every day after school to watch the practices. He knew every player's name, every coach. He knew his dad had been interviewed for the vacant head coach job. He knew he had a chance to get it.

"I was really hoping for him. I mean I was really into it," says Jimmy, who a little more than a decade later would play for his father on BYU's national championship team.

"He said he'd tell me as soon as he found out anything. And you know what? That's exactly what he did."

• • •

Ann Edwards was satisfied that she'd milked as much sympathy as possible out of the fact she would be going to the dance alone. She'd told her friends. She'd told her church leaders. She'd told the people planning the food.

She would not be bringing a date to daddy-daughter night.

Her dad was a football coach, and in the winter that meant he was on the road recruiting players. She didn't know where he was but she knew where he wasn't. He wasn't home. He'd left on his current trip about a week earlier and wouldn't be back for at least another week. She'd have to go to the dance alone. At age eleven, she'd accepted reality. And was making sure everybody knew it.

"I'd already gone through my sob story," says

Ann, now a parent herself and an award-winning writer of children's books. "I got as many people to feel sorry for me as I could. I'd told everyone that my father couldn't make it."

Then the night of the dance came—and so did her father.

"He walked through the door just before it started and said, 'We're going,'" says Ann.

She had a date.

It would be a one-night stand. LaVell Edwards had interrupted his recruiting trip for this detour back home. He'd bought a ticket at the airport in Los Angeles, flown to Salt Lake City, and then driven to Provo. The next morning he'd fly back to L.A.

"It wasn't treated like a huge production or anything," says Ann. "My mom—and she's no doubt the one who told him this would mean a lot to me—didn't say, 'Look what your father did for you,' and neither did he. I'm sure they couldn't really afford it and it was a big hassle. But I didn't know that then. All I knew was I was so glad to see him.

"There wasn't anything particularly memorable about the dance. We did some square dancing, I'm sure they had the usual dry roast beef and the Jell-O salad, and I was probably a lousy date. But it meant a lot to me to have him there. It always meant a lot to me when he was there, and he had this way of knowing when it was important that he be there.

"I've thought about that as I've gotten older and people have analyzed the way he coaches. He doesn't wear the headset and kind of stands around and they wonder how much he's involved. But then you talk to his players and they say he's always there when they need him. I find myself thinking, 'He treats his players the way he treated me.'

"I always liked my dad. You know how kids go through a time when they don't like their parents—well, that never happened with me."

• • •

John Edwards tried out the power windows. He adjusted the power seat. He turned up the stereo cassette player. He adjusted the climate control. Now *this* was a car.

He was on the I-15 freeway, cruising to an appointment in Salt Lake City in his dad's new Mercury—a Cougar, of course. The appointment was important to him, and while talking about it the night before he'd said something about hoping his car, a 1964 Volkswagen bug, would make it. His dad said why not take his car and he'd drive John's car to the football office, where he worked.

If it hadn't been for the cracked windshield, the expired plates, the bumper tied on by a shoelace, the expired registration—and the sharp eye of the BYU security patrolman who turned on his lights and pulled him over—his dad might have actually made it to work.

"I'm sure the security guy who pulled him over figured he'd hit the jackpot," says John, still enjoying that crime scene as he imagines it almost twenty years later. "Here's this car driving through campus with everything wrong. He pulls it over . . . and then out steps my dad.

"Neither one of them knew what to say."

"My dad started to chew me out when he got home that night," says John, now an orthopedic surgeon with children of his own—who themselves will soon be driving. "But then he just started laughing.

"That's the way he is. He'll give you anything he has. And if there are consequences, well, he deals with them.

"But he isn't bad at taking, either," John is quick to add. "I know I'd be a wealthy man if I had a dollar for every chocolate sundae I made on a Sunday night and he came in and grabbed it and said, 'Now make one for yourself.' He's a man who knows how to give . . . and how to receive."

CHAPTER THREE

Perspective

Tommy Briggs was a great kid. He was outgoing and popular. He was a student body officer at his high school, he was an outstanding tennis player, and he came from a great family that included his father, Mel, and his mother, Jean. Mel and Jean hadn't had Tommy until later on in their marriage, after they thought children might not be possible. When Tommy did come along, the event did not go unappreciated. Talk about parents who really enjoy raising a son, and a son who enjoyed it just as much in return— that was the Briggses.

Then Tommy came down with leukemia.

The cancer attacked from out of nowhere, and within a matter of months Tommy was in and out of hospitals, fighting, at the age of eighteen, for his life.

I got a call from his father one night during a particularly hard time. He said Tommy was in the hospital in Salt Lake, and he wondered if I could find time to pay him a visit. I said I would.

I'd do anything I could for Mel Briggs. He was my high school basketball coach and had always been a positive influence in my life. It was Mel who got me excited about going on to college when I was still in high school—and since he went to Utah State, I'm sure that helped influence my decision to go to Utah State.

But finding the time to visit Tommy wasn't going to be easy. This was in 1972, early in my first season as BYU's head football coach, and not having enough time was just one of the things I was worrying about. You name it, I was uptight about it. Taking over a college program was a new experience for me, and I was feeling all kinds of new pressures—both from within and without.

We'd gotten lucky and won our first game against Kansas State, and in our fourth game we'd gone to Los Angeles and beaten Long Beach State in Anaheim Stadium. Long Beach had a great running back named Terry Metcalf, so that made that win all the better. Our own great running back, Pete Van Valkenburg, was leading the nation in rushing. People were starting to show more than a passing interest in what we were doing. Our next game was against the University of Texas–El Paso (UTEP) in Provo. It was homecoming and the game was getting a lot of attention. Tommy Hudspeth had gone from BYU to the staff at UTEP, so he'd be coaching for the first time against his old school—a factor that added yet another dimension to the game. Nobody wanted to lose this one.

I was a nervous wreck more or less around the clock. All I could think about was football, football, football. My mind was cluttered. I was having trouble sleeping. The worrying alone was a full-time job.

It wasn't until the Thursday night before the UTEP game that I found the time to go to the hospital in Salt Lake to see Tommy—and even then I was just squeezing it in. Mel had said my visit would mean a lot to Tommy because he'd followed the news of me becoming BYU's new coach closely. He knew I'd played for his dad in high school and he thought that was great. Not long into our visit it became obvious that Tommy knew all about our players and everything about our season to that point. It seemed he knew more about BYU football than I did. He wasn't just a fan; he was a huge fan. He had pictures and articles all around his hospital room, which he showed to me, and he talked with great enthusiasm about the game coming up that Saturday.

The whole time I was there his focus was BYU football. Other than us beating UTEP, it was as if he didn't have a care in the world. He called me "coach." He told me how glad he was I'd had the time to visit. He was a really happy kid.

As I drove back to Provo that night with my wife, Patti, I remember talking about Tommy's attitude and what an inspiration it had been. As we talked, it dawned on me more and more that there are a lot of things in life you can worry about. You can choose to spend all your time worrying about them, or you can choose not to give them any more attention than they deserve. You can choose to focus as much as you possibly can on those things that are positive and beneficial. That's what I'd seen Tommy Briggs do that night in the hospital. He could have spent an hour talking about his cancer, about his misfortunes, about having to be in that bed instead of on a tennis court, but instead he chose to talk about something that brought him pleasure.

Tommy died not long after that. But he left a lasting impact on me. He gave me a valuable lesson in perspective—and at a critical point in my life. At the rate I was going midway through that first season as head coach, I honestly don't know how long I would have lasted.

I will never completely get over my penchant for worrying, of course. If they ever make worrying a medal sport in the Olympics, I know I could be a contender. But I have become much better at sorting out what I will worry about, and when. I recognize how senseless it is to worry about things you don't have control over, and that even when it comes to things you do have some control over, you can't dwell on them all the time.

No matter what your job, it will consume you if you let it. I know that's true when your job is directing a college football program. There are so many things to deal with, so many things I hadn't even imagined before becoming a head coach. Indulging even half of them could drive you out of your mind. You'd wind up working eighteen hours a day, and then finally you'd burn out and wonder what happened.

For example, officiating, all by itself, could drive a coach out of the football business. It happens. I've seen it happen. That's why I've made it a personal point not to worry about officiating—at least as much as is humanly possible. I have my times when I question a referee's eyesight. I've gotten upset over more than one call. But that's where it stops. I make a conscious effort to not get hung up over officiating, to not take it home with me, or to not take it into the next game. I don't have any real control over it. All my worrying about it will just make me more upset.

I used to think if I could ever get rid of my current big problem (whatever it was), then I wouldn't have anything to worry about. But things obviously don't work that way. I'm always going to have problems to deal with. Everyone is. That's life. The trick is in keeping the problems manageable and in a proper perspective. The trick is in managing the problems and not letting the problems manage you.

The only effective way to do that is by developing a healthy perspective.

WHERE FAMILY FITS

More than anything else, I think it's our families that help keep our perspectives square. They keep us balanced. I know that's been my personal experience. There's no telling where I'd be or how I'd have turned out without both of my families—the one that raised me and the one I've helped raise. If I've been able to maintain something of an even keel over the years, and not go overboard either way about where I've been or what I've done, it's because of them, not me. They get the credit. If I've ever gone too far in one direction, there's always been someone there to rein me in.

My married life started that way.

I met Patti when she was a freshman at Utah State and I was a junior. The school year had just begun, football season was underway, and tryouts for the Sponsor Corps were taking place in the football stadium.

The Sponsor Corps was a women's marching group at Utah State that carried rifles and pom-poms and performed at halftime at basketball games; it was the forerunner to the Aggiettes of today. One of the girls trying out was Patti Covey of Big Piney, Wyoming. I was in the ROTC, and because of that I was one of the judges assigned to select the girls who would make the Sponsor Corps. I had no real qualifications for this duty, other than the ability to recognize a cute girl when I saw one.

The afternoon after I first saw Patti, I asked a friend of mine who was dating Patti's girlfriend to line us up. I said to be sure to mention that I'd voted for her for Sponsor Corps. Within a week we went on our first date. It was a Saturday night after a home football game. I was impressed because all night long Patti not only kept talking about football, but she talked specifically about the positions I played.

This made a big impact on me because I was a linebacker and a center. When you're a linebacker not a lot of people notice what you're doing, and when you're a center no one outside of your mother notices. But Patti did, and all that fall, as we got more and more serious, she talked each week about my performance as a football player.

The next spring I gave her my fraternity pin, and by the time school was out I gave her an engagement ring. We had our wedding in the middle of the summer.

After a reception in Wyoming we went on our honeymoon to Sun Valley. Her parents gave us a new car, a 1951 Chevrolet Bel Air coupe, and as we drove in it toward Sun Valley Patti got this serious look on her face and said, "I think it's important that we're always very honest with each other in our marriage." I told her I agreed with that, absolutely, and then she confessed: She said she'd never actually seen me play football.

She said she didn't even really like football—but she had a friend who did. Through the entire previous season it had been her friend who had gone to the games and watched me play. Afterward, she'd give Patti a briefing, like somebody giving you notes for a history class you missed, so she could impress me when we went out that night.

That said, she settled back in her seat and said she felt much better. I've never really let her forget that she didn't come clean until *after* the wedding.

I've always had people around me to keep me humble. When our daughter, Ann, was attending BYU and was doing particularly well in an English class, I said to her, "Well, Ann, do they know who you are?"

"Dad," she answered, "I would never tell them anything like that!"

"I'm not trying to help you," I said. "I'm trying to help my own image."

Patti and I have been fortunate to have three very independent, very responsible children. Ann is a writer, John is a doctor, and Jimmy is a lawyer. Their professions provide a pretty good clue as to their individuality. None of them stayed with the family business of coaching football, although Jimmy did show some early interest, an interest I have to admit I discouraged more than I encouraged. That's probably because I know I've been luckier than most coaches in being able to stay in one place most of my career. I knew there was no guarantee that the same would hold true for Jimmy.

But it's not that I ever tried to talk him out of coaching. Or out of anything else. We always wanted the children to make their own choices and chart their own way. When they were growing up we were lucky to live in a great neighborhood with a lot of good families that provided a healthy environment—so we were able to make that available to them. As for athletics, I never wanted any of the kids to feel like they had to participate because I was a coach, and that included playing football. It's funny the way it all worked out. John played football and ran track in high school, and then elected to stick to track in college. Jimmy, on the other hand, decided not to play football his sophomore year in high school, then reconsidered and played football his last two years of high school before playing at BYU.

When Jimmy came to me and said he wasn't going out for high school football as a sophomore, I told him that was no problem for me, no problem at all. And it wasn't. Just as it was no problem when he changed his mind a year later.

When Jimmy played for me at BYU I'm sure it could have been a problem. I've heard my share of nightmare stories about father-son coaching-playing experiences. The team can give the coach's son a hard time just because he is the coach's son. There can be jealousies. The coach can bend over backwards to be hard on his own son, or he can show favoritism to him. And on and on.

But Jimmy ended up playing four seasons as a receiver—he started some games as a senior—and there were no problems at all. None. Going in, we never did talk specifically about how we were going to handle it. We just let it unfold the way it would. I have to give Jimmy a lot of credit. He handled the situation well. He made it easy. Looking back, I'd have to say one thing that helped is that neither of us had any preconceived agendas about what had to happen. There were no mandates, either way, that he had to do this or he had to do that. Basically all Jimmy did was show up and play football—and it worked out.

I was never one to give lectures or advice. While the kids were growing up I didn't specifically talk about the family being our top priority, or that they should do this or do that. I did try to give them enough of my time so they would know they were important to me. There were times when I'd leave work—both when I was an assistant coach and when I was the head coach—to take care of some particular problem or situation with the family. I didn't do it at the expense of the program, and I didn't do it because the problem or situation was necessarily all that important. I did it because I sensed it was important to the person involved; I felt that my presence at that time was important to them. Just being there is often what really matters—letting others know that you're someone they can talk to and count on.

I wasn't always there. There were times when I'd get preoccupied and then look back and wish I'd put aside what I was doing long enough to take care of my family responsibilities. But I always tried to keep the right priorities because I know those little things have a way of being cumulative, and as they build up they create good relationships. We've never had relationship problems with any of our children, which amazes me to this day. But it's true, and I'd have to guess that just being there is probably the biggest reason why.

Giving them time is important. It's not easy. You have to work at it. But time is time. Whether you're gone to a church meeting or playing golf, all your kids know is that you're gone. They don't differentiate.

It was an advantage for me as a young head coach to have a family, in addition to my team, to take care of. So many times, the two "jobs" merged into one, and I think both were better off as a result. Whenever we could, we'd get in the car as a family and drive to coaching clinics I wanted to attend, or to coaching conventions, or on recruiting trips. We saw much of the country that way, and I know it helped our family grow closer together. We'd get one motel room and just cram in there. Those memories are some of the best I have.

In later years, after we'd had a lot of success as a football program and after the kids were gone, we'd go to bowl games and they'd put us in these huge hotel suites and Patti and I would look at each other and wonder, "Where was this when we needed it?"

It would be difficult for me to overstate the positive influence Patti has had on me and on our family. When I couldn't be there for the children, she always was. She's always had a great capacity to smooth out the edges and make things run well, and her support has been the kind that any football coach needs from his wife.

That "support" gained national attention in 1986, after we'd played UCLA in the Freedom Bowl to end the season. UCLA beat us 31–10 in that game, scoring the final touchdown on a halfback pass late in the game. As a card-carrying member of the Football Writers Association—because of the column she wrote for the *Provo Daily Herald*—Patti attended the post-game press conference. When Terry Donahue, the UCLA coach, came to the podium she raised her hand and asked if he really felt it was necessary to boost his score by throwing that halfback pass that late in the game.

Needless to say, when the identity of the person asking the question came to light, there was a bit of a stir. The story appeared in any number of newspapers around the country the next day, and in the following week's editions of *Newsweek* and *Sports Illustrated*.

One of Patti's greatest assets is a marvelous sense of humor. A couple of winters ago she gave me a snowblower for Christmas. But since I still like to shovel the snow by hand, I returned the snowblower and bought a compact disc player instead. A few weeks later, after a heavy snowstorm, I was shoveling the drive in the early morning. As I was mumbling to myself about all that snow, Patti opened the front door and asked if I would like her to turn up the CD player.

THERE'S MORE TO LIFE THAN FOOTBALL

Besides having a supportive family life to help me keep my perspective and priorities in order, I have also learned to lean a lot on outside interests.

I don't care what the profession, diversity is important. I've always had interests beyond football. I love to read books, especially in the off season. I enjoy seeing movies. I like all kinds of music, with Willie Nelson's just a notch ahead of Mozart's.

Any kind of healthy diversion is, well, healthy. I happen to iron my own clothes. I find that ironing is therapeutic for me. I'll iron during the season. I've even ironed during two-a-days—but not so anyone could see.

My two biggest personal diversions over the years have been—and here's a contrast for you—flowers and golf.

I guess what they say is true: You can take the farmer out of the farm but you can't take the farm out of the farmer. I've always taken a lot of pride in growing and taking care of the flowers around our house. Anyone who comes to the house is sooner or later going to be asked if they noticed the flowers.

Golf is probably the most consistently challenging thing I've ever done. People say, "Why play golf? You've got enough frustrations." And I say that it's nice to get frustrated about something besides what normally gets you frustrated.

Golf for me is an escape as much as it is a challenge. It gives me a chance to compete away from the football field, and I love to compete. For years basketball was my favorite competitive outlet. If I hadn't hurt my knee in the army I'm sure I would have played basketball a lot longer. When I couldn't, golf took over.

One of the few regrets I have in life is that I didn't learn the mechanics of the golf swing earlier. You just can't go back and make up for that lost time. Especially if you don't practice, which I almost never do. I like to play a game and I like to compete. For me, those are golf's addictive attractions. I don't ever play alone, and I prefer not to play "company" golf. I like to play with people I like to play with. Put me on a golf course with good friends and some kind of game and I can completely forget what I do for a living. It's a great outlet from football. And if I miss an important putt, I can go home from a golf game every bit as frustrated as I can after a football game.

Another therapy I've found particularly effective over the years has been having someone to talk to. One of the reasons I hated to see Dick Felt retire following our 1993 season was that in addition to being a great coach, Dick was such a great friend to talk to. We coached together for thirty years. We shared an office when we were both assistants. We've probably played a thousand rounds of golf together. With Dick I had someone close I could tell anything to, and he'd listen. He was a perfect sounding board. Sometimes that's all you need. You don't necessarily need advice or help. Most of the time you're going to work your problems out on your own anyway. But you do need a good friend to listen to what's on your mind. I don't talk a lot. I'm really quite self-contained. But I still need to talk sometimes. I need that outlet as much as anyone else.

Dick hasn't always agreed with what I've had to say. I found that out the first time I met him, when he was a senior at Lehi High School in 1951. Dick was an outstanding high school athlete, and all of the Utah schools were recruiting him. Because I was from Orem, the coaches at Utah State asked me to go with them when they drove to Lehi to recruit Dick. I was a senior at Utah State at the time. I told Dick how great it was at Utah State and how much he'd enjoy playing football there. I told him the only time I got in trouble was when I came home in the summers and hung out with the BYU guys.

The next thing I heard he'd signed with BYU.

Another important part of my life that has helped my perspective is my faith. The importance the gospel of Jesus Christ places on families, and on the worship of God, puts pursuits such as football in their proper priority. It isn't that football—or any cause we might choose to pursue—is insignificant. Rather, it's that the gospel helps define its place. Your profession should never be served to the exclusion of other important things in life.

Church callings have a way of keeping you from spending inordinately long hours in the office or the film room. Not long after I came to BYU I was called to be the bishop of a student ward on campus. That experience proved to be a valuable one in many ways. One lesson I learned, and didn't expect to, was that the things that worked in dealing with students in the ward also worked in dealing with students on the football team.

Our kids were little when I was a bishop. I remember one fast and testimony meeting when a girl who had recently worked out some personal problems stood up to bear her testimony. She'd gone through the repentance process, and as her bishop I'd tried to help by offering as much spiritual counsel as I could. In her testimony she expressed how grateful she was for the gospel and for the principle of repentance. She was quite emotional by the time she got to the part about how grateful she was "for Bishop Edwards, a true man of God, a man," she said, "who always makes you feel good because no matter what you've done he'll understand because he's already done it."

I looked down from the stand at Pat and our three kids sitting there on the front row—all of them looking up at me with these what-did-she-mean-by-that? looks on their faces.

Our families are truly our greatest assets. They help us chart our course. They help keep us going in the right direction. They keep our perspectives on course. They're easily the best hedge I know of for runaway egos. In that department, where my own kids left off, my grandchildren have capably picked up. Recently I was in Bountiful, watching John's son, Matt, play in a Little League baseball game. After the game a bunch of the boys on the two teams came over to where I was sitting to ask for my autograph. As I was signing my name, I overheard one of them ask Matt, who was standing off to the side, if he was going to get "Coach Edwards' autograph."

"Naw," Matt said, "He's just my grandpa."

Just That Side of Normal

From a man who was recruited by him, who played for him, and who has coached for him practically ever since:

"LaVell Edwards," says Lance Reynolds, "is not normal."

He searches for a better word.

"He's . . . different."

Reynolds saw the differences early, and over the years he's seen them often. If you've got the time, he's got the stories.

ON RECRUITING

"They used to have two letters of intent, one for the conference and one nationally. You could sign several conference letters but just one national letter. That was your final choice. I had signed a conference letter with BYU, but I'd decided I'd sign the national letter with the University of California at Berkeley. I was very impressed by Mike White, Cal's head coach. He wore three-piece suits; he had a Rolex; he was polished; he said all the right things; he brought a book about Cal to the house when he met my parents, a book he'd helped write. A picture-perfect recruiter.

"In those days it was legal to take a recruit out to dinner. Mike White had come to town and taken me to dinner at this really nice, very expensive restaurant. After that I was Cal's. I signed their letter. All I had to do was put it in the mail. When my dad came home that night I told him. He didn't say anything, but he called LaVell. The next morning I got a call from LaVell—I didn't know how he had found out—and he said, 'Please don't sign anything until we can talk.' He said he'd drive up that night and we'd go out to dinner. So LaVell drove up and we talked, and the more we talked the more I got this feeling: This is the man I want to play for. He's not slick like Mike White, but something tells me that if I'm hurt or something goes wrong, he'll take care of me. I just got that feeling. So I changed my mind, and I'm thinking, 'All right, now let's go to dinner. I wonder where he's going to take me.' We got in his car and drove up the street and he pulled into a McDonald's. Mike White took me to the nicest place in town and LaVell fed me a burger and took me home."

ON WHOSE TEAM IT IS

"Nearly every coach I've been around has acted like a boss. Everything is theirs. Normally a coach talks to his team at the beginning of the season and he'll say, 'This is my team, and we're going to do it my way.' LaVell doesn't handle it that way at all. LaVell says, 'This is your football team, and for you seniors, it's your last football team. You decide how far you want to go.' It's a totally different approach. You're not going to find it many places. Players and coaches at BYU need to motivate from within. Nothing about LaVell says, 'I'm going to drive you, I'm going to threaten you, I'm going to make you fear me.'"

ON MOTIVATION

"We're playing at Arizona my senior year. We're coming off a big win over Colorado State, and we know if we can beat Arizona we'll be in the driver's seat for the conference championship. In the first half we'd struggled offensively but were still up by two or three points.

"LaVell assembled us together and said, 'If we can hang on we'll be in great shape. Everybody will be chasing us.' Just what you'd expect him to say. But then he added, 'If we lose, we're not out of it. But we're going to have to play well the rest of the season.' It wasn't like 'We've got to win or else.' He just laid it on the line like it was. We went out and won, but we didn't feel like we had to."

MORE ON MOTIVATION

"Remember Casey Tiamalu? He was a blood-and-guts guy, a real warrior. Personality wise, that's the way he played. He liked to get real pumped up. He used to want fiery speeches from LaVell. One halftime we walked in and Casey couldn't take it any longer. He shouted, 'Hey, LaVell, tell them to get it up! Let's get them fired up!' He actually did that. He called him LaVell. I'm thinking, 'Oh, man.' But LaVell didn't miss a beat. He just went on with his usual speech.

"He knows the kind of mood he wants to set for the team. His approach says, 'Instead of being emotional, be good.' If you're good you'll win most of the time. If you're emotional you might win once in a while. I think that's one of the reasons we're more consistent than most places."

ON WORKING FOR HIM

"I coach the running backs and I have a lot of freedom. All the coaches do. Nobody looks over our shoulders and tells us what has to be done. But it's a different freedom from what people might think. If a head coach comes in and constantly tells you exactly what you have to do, then it's not really your area and you're not going to feel as responsible for it. But if you feel like it is your area, then you are going to feel more responsible for what goes on, and you're going to be more motivated to be creative and good.

"LaVell's not the kind of guy who will get on you if you make a mistake. If it's deliberate, he will. More than people know, he'll get after you. But if you call a play and you're honestly doing the best job you can, he's not the kind of guy who will send a message that you shouldn't have done that. He will talk to you. Say we're in a group out on the field and he sees something. He'll pull you off to the side and he'll say, 'Now what would you think of this?' But he won't ever say, 'Now that was a stupid idea.'

"Sometimes you don't even know he's around. Out on the field he rarely says anything to me. He watches a lot. Most head coaches, when they walk up to a drill, will take the drill over. He doesn't. You're the coach. And he doesn't second-guess you. Listen to him on the radio. Suppose something did go wrong in a game in a particular coach's area. LaVell won't bring it up in public. He'll never make a deliberate attack on a coach or on a player. We may have a quarterback who's real average. LaVell will never say that, even though it's the truth and it may be the problem. He'll just say that we're going to work on our game, without naming names. He doesn't blame others. He calls on your personal pride. You perform because you want to, not because he wants you to."

ON HIS COUNSEL

"His door is always open. He'll talk to you about whatever's on your mind. But he's not going to fix it. You can go in there with a major problem, all fired up and determined to get his help on what to do. So you sit down and talk, and when you get up and leave you're feeling better. But then you think, 'Now wait a minute, what did he tell me I should do? He didn't tell me anything!' He's eased your mind. He's calmed you down. But you've still got your problem. Then you decide, 'Well, since he didn't take care of it for me, I'll go take care of it myself.'"

IN SUMMARY

"It would drive some guys crazy working for him. Some guys want all their instructions on a sheet of paper—they want to know exactly how everything is organized and who reports to whom and who's responsible for what. They're most comfortable when the head coach has all the answers. They prefer to work for someone who handles all the problems.

"But I wouldn't."

CHAPTER FOUR

How I Came to Pass

I am often asked what was behind my decision for BYU to try the forward pass.

Frustration had a lot to do with it.

If BYU football had been on a winning roll when I was hired as head coach, I wouldn't have had any compelling desire to try anything new. I have no personal argument with success. I have no lifelong quest to go against the flow. I'd been a conservative, run-oriented football coach to that point of my career, and I would have happily remained a conservative, run-oriented football coach. Who was I to argue in the face of Woody Hayes and three-yards-and-a-cloud-of-dust?

But there was a sense of urgency about BYU football, a sense of urgency with a center of gravity, I soon realized, that was anchored in the chair of the head coach. I felt something had to be done, and preferably done fast. I remember hearing rumors that the school might not want to keep fielding football teams if success continued to be so elusive. I never personally checked any of those rumors out. Probably because I didn't want to know the answer.

In 1972 I was perfectly willing to accept the fact that I had inherited something of a problem child.

I'd been an assistant coach at BYU for ten seasons, so I knew of the school's frustrating history with football. The Western Athletic Conference championship we'd won in 1965 was the only championship BYU had ever won. Period. That was it. One league championship in school history. I was also well aware of BYU's status as a private religious school, and as with all private schools, that carried with it its own restrictions and limitations when it came to recruiting and admissions.

Fortunately, I had a pretty good idea of what BYU was and what BYU wasn't. I knew the purposes behind the honor code that all incoming students—football players included—were required to observe. I was a lifelong member of the church that owned the school. I'd grown up within a few orchards of the campus.

I knew the hand I'd been dealt, in other words. I knew what I had to work with and what I didn't have to work with—and I had no real problems accepting any of it. I'd have to say that having that kind of inside information and being okay with it was essentially my biggest plus.

Given those circumstances, I decided for the simplest of reasons that I wanted to have an offense that was wide open. If we didn't, I didn't think we could win.

We just didn't have the personnel for a grind-it-out running attack, which was the favored offense of the day. Typically, the best running backs went to the best programs, and we weren't one of them. We were basically left with running backs we hoped would develop into major college quality—as was the case with Pete Van Valkenburg in 1972. But to expect that to happen every year was asking a lot.

In the '60s and into the '70s, the run was the thing in college football. You either ran out of the power-I, as they did at Ohio State, Michigan, Notre Dame, Southern Cal, and so on, or you ran out of the wishbone, as was favored by, among others, Oklahoma, Alabama, Arkansas, and Texas. Those were primarily your two choices. Anything else was bucking the system. Passing was basically used as a way to keep defenses honest, and only occasionally, much like an off-speed pitch in baseball.

Every now and then a school would use the pass to try to jump-start a struggling program. San Jose State, for instance, tried the pass in the '50s, when Bob Bronzan was the head coach and a young graduate assistant named Bill Walsh was part of his staff. At BYU, for another example, we'd gone to a predominant passing approach when Virgil Carter was the quarterback in 1965 and 1966. Until Bronzan left in

1957, San Jose State had a winning record, as we did at BYU behind Virgil Carter's arm.

Probably the most successful "passing experiment" came at Stanford, where head coach John Ralston went from a basic run to a basic pass offense and, behind quarterbacks Don Bunce and Jim Plunkett, won consecutive Rose Bowls at the end of both the 1970 and 1971 seasons. Ralston's success had a particularly big impact on me because I'd known John when he coached at Utah State—before he left for Stanford—and I knew his preference was for a running attack. But after assessing his personnel at Stanford he'd decided—correctly, as it turned out—that a passing offense would give him a better chance to succeed.

I knew that in many ways, Stanford and BYU were alike. Both were private schools with their own peculiar recruiting problems. I remember thinking that if Stanford could have success with the pass, if they could use it to move out of the estimable shadows of UCLA and USC and make it to the Rose Bowl, maybe the same thing could work for BYU. The success we'd had with Virgil Carter in the '60s, when we won our only championship, made me think that way even more.

TRYING SOMETHING DIFFERENT

As I began preparing for my first spring practice as a head coach in 1972, I decided that if the ship went down, I at least wanted it to go down trying something different. It was why my first hiring decision was to offer the job of quarterback coach/offensive coordinator to Don Rydalch, the head coach at Ricks College in Rexburg, Idaho. Don had the credentials I was looking for. He'd been a quarterback himself. He'd played for Jack Curtice at the University of Utah when Curtice's offenses were among the most wide open in the country. At Ricks, his teams threw the ball almost as much as they ran it. I suspected he would be willing to open up even more at BYU.

He initially accepted my offer. But when Don got in his car to drive to Provo for the start of spring ball, he made it only a few miles out of town. His car skidded on some ice covering the Madison Bridge; and instead of arriving at spring practice in Provo, he landed in the Rexburg Memorial Hospital. While he was laid up, Don decided he'd stay and convalesce at Ricks.

Offensively, that left us somewhat shorthanded for our first spring practice. But naiveté was a plus in this case. We'd never had much, so we didn't know what we were missing. It wasn't until spring ball was over that I got around to filling the quarterback coach position. The coach I wound up hiring had even fewer credentials than I did.

Dewey Warren, a.k.a. "The Swamp Rat," was a twenty-eight-year-old assistant freshman football coach at his alma mater, the University of Tennessee, when we brought him to Provo in the late spring of 1972 as BYU's new quarterback coach. Dewey and one of my defensive coaches, Jim Criner, had become acquainted when Jim went to Tennessee to observe a special "bubble defense" the Volunteers were using.

To say the least, Dewey's coaching experience was limited. He was just a couple of years removed from his playing days. He had been an All-American quarterback at Tennessee and then spent a short time in the pros, with the Cincinnati Bengals and the Las Vegas Cowboys, before joining the Tennessee staff to help out with their freshman team. In those days there were no restrictions on staff size and some of the bigger schools, especially in the South, had fifteen or sixteen coaches. At Tennessee in 1972, the Swamp Rat was one of a crowd. It was probably mid-season before they even knew he was gone.

Dewey wound up staying just two years in Provo, but that was long enough. It was his familiarity with throwing the football—or "thowing," as he twanged it—that brought the pass to Provo.

The circumstances really couldn't have been better for change. I knew almost nothing about a passing offense. For the previous eight years I'd been BYU's defensive coordinator, and before that I'd worked with BYU and Granite High on only one offense, the now-defunct single wing. On the other hand, about the only thing Dewey Warren knew was passing. He loved to throw the ball. The only thing he could coach was the only thing we couldn't.

So I got out of the Swamp Rat's way and he set up a "thowing" offense for BYU. What he gave us wasn't revolutionary. He drew us up a basic passing game out of the pro formation. It was essentially what was called the pro attack, with both the wingback and the split end sent wide. They were doing quite a bit of that by then in professional football. In the pro attack you still had two backs in the backfield and a tight end. The difference was those two players who were sent wide—the wingback and split end. Later, they would be called "wide receivers."

Dewey had played the pro attack. He understood it. He knew how to block for it, how to run the pass routes, how far to drop back—he knew all of that. Which was a good thing, since nobody else did.

The players and the staff took to Dewey from the start. His talk about "thowing" got everyone excited. But since he didn't get a chance to work with the team until August drills, since we didn't have any quarterbacks whose skills fit the pro attack, and since we had a running back, Pete Van Valkenburg, who was good enough to lead the nation in rushing in 1972, it was a year before we got around to his passing plans. It wasn't until the 1973 season that we actually tried out the offense he'd set up. When we did, it was primarily because of a recruit who came to us on the rebound.

Gary Sheide was an outstanding all-around athlete at Antioch High School in northern California whom I'd tried to recruit when I was an assistant to Tommy Hudspeth. Several other major colleges were also interested in him, but he turned all the football offers down because he wanted to play baseball instead. He went to Diablo Valley, a junior college near his hometown, to play shortstop for the baseball team in the hopes that he could go on to play professionally.

That might have been that if prior to the football season both of Diablo Valley's quarterbacks hadn't gone down with injuries. Gary, an outstanding high school quarterback who looked just like Joe Namath, slouch and all, was asked to fill in. He said he would on condition that nobody could hit him in practice and he could pass as much as he wanted.

Diablo Valley won its first three games before Gary broke his right wrist, an injury that kept him out of the baseball season—and, because of that, that summer's professional baseball draft. By the next fall he was back playing football. Again Diablo Valley won its first three games and again Gary, a right-hander, broke his right wrist.

I wasn't aware any of this was going on. As far as I knew, Gary Sheide was playing baseball somewhere—until Jim Criner came into the office one day and recommended we take a look at a junior college quarterback named Gary Sheide. He said Sheide was injured, but he'd never lost a game in junior college and he liked to throw the ball, which of course is what we were looking for.

We decided to go after him again, for the second time, and he came up for a visit midway through the season. It was one of those beautiful fall Saturdays in Provo. The leaves were changing, the air was crisp, we had a good crowd in the stadium, and we were really on for our game that day. We won and Gary got excited about coming to BYU. Later on, a number of other schools recruited him heavily, but we had the inside track and he chose to play at Brigham Young, where he asked for jersey number 12, Joe Namath's number.

Dewey Warren and Gary Sheide were the first two key pieces of the passing puzzle we were trying to put together. The third was a wide receiver out of northern California named Jay Miller, who was also recruited by Jim Criner. (Without Jim Criner, the BYU passing attack may never have gotten off the ground: He's the one who found Dewey Warren, he's the one who found Gary Sheide, and he's the one who recruited Jay Miller. Ironically, he was a defensive coach.) Jay was an outstanding receiver who would catch one hundred passes in 1973, the first season he teamed up with Gary, setting an NCAA record that wouldn't be broken for many years. In just one game that season, against New Mexico, he caught twenty-two passes for another NCAA record.

With our 1972 rushing champion (Van Valkenburg) graduated, and with Sheide and Miller in camp, we plugged in Dewey Warren's offense for the entire 1973 season. For the first time ever, BYU was noticeably different on offense.

It did take us a while to loosen the constraints of half a century of traditional football. In the first three games—against Colorado State, Oregon State, and Utah State—we started first Dave Terry and then Randy Litchfield at quarterback. Gary had pulled a groin muscle in August two-a-days and began the season on crutches. In the third game, against Utah State, he played the final minute and completed six of ten passes on a wild drive that ended on the five-yard line and almost pulled victory out of a 13–7 loss. That won him the starting job for the season's fourth game, our homecoming game against Iowa State.

It was in that 26–24 loss to the Cyclones that the BYU passing game had its real debut. Dewey Warren turned Gary Sheide loose, and he responded with 439 yards, three touchdowns, and twenty-nine completions in forty-one attempts. The passing era would have begun with a win if a last-second field goal hadn't gone wide. But whatever the outcome, one thing was certain: It had begun.

It's easy now to look back and see what in 1973 wasn't so clear. Back then we weren't trying to reinvent the game; we were just trying to win football games. And as eye-popping as those passing statistics were after the Iowa State game, we were still a 1-and-3 football team that would soon be 1-and-5 after consecutive road losses to Arizona State and Wyoming. I have wondered many times why I stuck so steadfastly to the passing game when it didn't translate into wins in the beginning—especially since we'd won seven games by running the ball just the season before.

But we did stick with it, and we managed to rebound with four wins in our final five games of the 1973 season. The passing game began to have its share of moments. We beat Utah in Salt Lake 46–22 when Gary threw four touchdown passes, and in the season finale we beat UTEP 63–0. Overall, Gary threw twenty-two touchdown passes in just eight starts, with only twelve interceptions.

All appeared to be going in the right direction heading into the 1974 season. Dewey Warren had gone to Kansas State, and we'd replaced him with an assistant coach from the College of San Mateo named Dwain Painter. We were still operating out of the offensive playbook drawn up by Dewey, but now it was according to Dwain's interpretations. Dwain was more of a traditional coach, and he favored more of a conservative look, adding options and rollouts to Dewey's fundamental pro attack.

We started the season with three tough losses, at Hawaii, against Utah State in Provo, and at Iowa State. We were still throwing the ball, but we weren't winning. For our fourth game, against Colorado State, we took out some of the options and rollouts and got Jay Miller, who'd been injured all fall, back into the lineup.

Things came back together, at least for a while. We were up 26–7 against the Rams until they caught fire and came back strong, pulling within a touchdown of the lead. Still, we were in good shape when we had the ball with a 33–27 lead, fifteen seconds left on the clock, and Colorado State out of timeouts. All we had to do was have Gary take the snap and touch a knee to win the game.

That proved easier said than done. The snap was bobbled and never made it to the quarterback. CSU recovered, and a coach's worst nightmare unfolded. In one play, the Rams scored, tied the game, and knew they could win it with an extra point.

That's when the bizarre ending got even more bizarre. Colorado State was penalized fifteen yards for coming onto the field to celebrate the touchdown, which was assessed on the extra-point try. The Rams' kicker was wide left. We left the field with a 33–33 tie, and I didn't know whether to laugh or cry.

We were 0–3–1, we'd just squandered a sure win, and I was as crushed as I ever would be as BYU's head coach. I wondered if we'd ever win another game. Worse than that, I wondered if I'd be around to see it. Before the Colorado State game, which was our conference opener, I'd made a strong pitch to the team, telling them that we hadn't lost a league game and we still had the potential for a championship and a successful year. Now I couldn't say that anymore. Frankly, I didn't know what to say.

As it turned out, I didn't have to say anything. After a couple of days and a lot of soul searching, two seniors on the team, Doug Adams and Mike Russell, came to my office and said they wanted to have a team meeting—and they didn't want it to include any of the coaches. They said there was quite a bit of turmoil and contention developing on the team, and they wanted to address it privately.

I told them, "Fine, have the meeting." So they did, and a lot of feelings got settled. From what I heard it was one of those "If you've got something to say, say it now and then that's it" kind of meetings. After they cleared the air, the players talked in terms of how much they loved each other, how much potential they felt the team had after the way the last season had ended, and how important it was to all of them to be part of something really good. They did this on their own, with the seniors taking the lead.

I've thought since how important that meeting was. It was just two guys on the team who took the lead—they weren't even captains—but after that things really came together. We had seven games left on our schedule, and we won all seven. We won the WAC title—only the second league championship in school history—and that got us an invitation to the first bowl game in the history of the school, the Fiesta Bowl in Tempe, Arizona. I believe we would have won that game—we lost 16–6—if Gary hadn't gotten hurt.

That season was as pivotal for me as it was for the passing game. If we hadn't pulled out of that 0–3–1 start, I'm not sure we'd have had the time we needed to get established.

Not that we were through with slow starts and growing pains. The next season we would also open with three defeats, and we almost added a fourth before our third-string quarterback pulled out a 16–15 win over New Mexico.

That third-string quarterback was a local kid from Provo High School named Gifford Nielsen. He was a sophomore in 1975, trying to decide between football and basketball, which he also played at BYU. After that New Mexico game we gave Gifford the start in the next game, against Air Force, and we won, 28–14. He started the rest of the year, and we were able to salvage another winning record, 6–5, despite another slow start. I wouldn't recommend that kind of pattern, although if you're going to have a slow time it's better to have it in September than November.

At the end of the season Dwain Painter took a job offer from UCLA. If nothing else, we were turning into a launching pad for quarterback coaches. Come to BYU and get a better job offer. Dwain's departure paved the way for the arrival of what would prove to be the BYU passing game's most significant ingredient.

Doug Scovil didn't come to campus wearing a professor's lab coat, but he could have.

Doug's most recent employer had been the San Francisco 49ers, where he was part of Dick Nolan's staff. When Nolan was fired, so was his staff, and that left Doug without a coaching job. It was during a conversation with Bill Walsh, whom I'd first met when he was an assistant to John Ralston at Stanford, that I learned about Doug Scovil. It was on Bill's recommendation that I contacted Doug about the opening we had for quarterback coach. Before he came to Provo we'd never met.

He impressed me immediately with his football knowledge— enough so that I offered him the job on the spot, at a salary of $19,000 a year. He said that wasn't much money and I said I agreed, but that was as far as I could stretch our 1977 salary budget. In many ways, Doug was overqualified for the position—the direct opposite of Dewey Warren. He was older, he was married, and he had extensive college and pro experience. He'd already been a head coach, and as the quarterback coach at the Naval Academy in 1963 he'd helped Roger Staubach win the Heisman Trophy.

I really didn't think we'd get him. But I called Bill Walsh, who was with the San Diego Chargers at the time, told him about my initial offer, and indicated that Doug had turned it down. Bill suggested that I not give up. He said to hold off for a while and then give Doug a call back. Considering the kind of football we were playing, he might reconsider despite the low pay.

I took that advice, and after going through spring practice without a quarterback coach—for the second time in five years—I again called Doug, who was still out of work. I said, "Look, why don't you just come and take a look at what we're doing? See if there might be something you'd like to do with it." That was my pitch. I didn't appeal to him with more money. I appealed to his artistic interests. I was essentially offering him an easel.

Well, it worked.

Doug came in and looked at our playbook and said, "Would you mind if I reorganized this a little bit, maybe just tied a few things together?" I told him to go ahead, and he was hooked.

The system we have now, in the '90s, is still basically the same system Doug Scovil set up in the mid '70s. That's when we started throwing to the backs. That's when we started to attack the seams. That's when we opened up. That's when it got crazy.

STAYING AHEAD OF THE DEFENSE

For about four or five years, we stayed ahead of the defenses. When everything worked it was really something—and it worked a lot. We were radically different from the norm, to say the least, and that made it hard for teams to prepare for us in just a week's time. They'd be used to practicing and preparing a certain way, they'd be comfortable with their routine, and then along would come the game with Brigham Young and all that passing. We were the thing you had to do once a year and hated, right up there with filing your tax return.

Doug Scovil had a brilliant football mind, and he was always using it. He was the kind of coach who wrote up plays on coffee shop napkins or drew them in the dirt. He dreamed about football. He was kind of a loner, in his own way, and somewhat eccentric. He tended to be secretive about what he was doing. He kept his desk locked. He was very protective. But he was a football soldier through and through, the kind of person you wanted to go to war with. When he died of a heart attack a few years ago, well before his time, he was on Buddy Ryan's staff with the Philadelphia Eagles. The Eagles players wore black arm patches in his honor the rest of the season.

Doug was as detail conscious as any coach I've ever known. He came to us just in time for Gifford Nielsen's junior season, and he immediately set to work fine-tuning the way Gifford played quarter-back. He worked on his footing, on his drop back, on his reading of defenses, on all kinds of little things you tend to forget or ignore—or, in some cases, not even know about. Doug was a perfectionist. With him, everything was precise. That included the pass routes and the pass blocking, as well as the quarterbacking. There was an exact way to run a route, and that was the only way it was to be run. The same went for pass blocking. Nowhere in the offense was there any room for casualness.

It was that penchant for exactness that sent us off on our passing wave in the '70s. It wasn't the big stuff as much as it was the little stuff: Sharp, crisp routes, precise blocking, disciplined reads. It's been that way ever since. Any success we've had is because we've stayed true to Doug Scovil's original principles of precision passing.

The fact that we were a step or two—and sometimes three—ahead of the posse didn't hurt in the beginning. In the '70s most teams were still basically playing a three-deep zone pass defense. In the three-deep, the weak safety is free to roam the middle, the strong safety locks on the tight end, the corners lock on the wide receivers, and the linebackers pick up the backs. There's nothing wrong with that defense, and teams still play it, but in the '70s they tended to play it almost exclusively, with very little change, and that's what Doug exploited. The whole concept of using the backs and the tight end as receivers, and then teaching the quarterback to know what to look for in all possible defensive reactions—in the beginning it was pure and simple exploitation.

Everything was set up to react to what the defense was doing. If you reacted correctly, there really wasn't anything the defense could do. The quarterback knew where the seams, or openings, would be, all depending on what the defense did. There were things a defense just couldn't stop. There still are, for that matter.

Over time, the defenses caught on and adjusted, of course. They always have and I'm sure they always will. But we have been able to continue to effectively throw the ball because it's proved to be a sound offense in its own right, fully capable of reacting to defensive shifts.

Like any sound offense, the passing game relies, in the final analysis, on execution more than on the element of surprise. People can know what you're doing and still not be able to stop it if you execute it right. Also, a key part of the system—more so than is generally perceived, I'm sure—has always been the running game. Any time we've had success, we've had a good running game as well as a good passing game.

The trigger to it all is the quarterback, of course. It's his decisions that make it go or not go. A popular question over the years has been whether the system makes the quarterback or the quarterback makes the system. The answer is boring, I know, but in reality it's a combination of both. The system isn't going to do much without a quarterback who knows how to run it, and a quarterback isn't going to do much until he knows the system.

The key is getting a quarterback who's going to use the system and put it ahead of his individual game. He has to be willing to work over and over again on getting the execution down. He has to be willing to play within its constraints.

We couldn't just stick anybody in at quarterback, and I believe we've proved that over the years. A lot more is required than just strength of arm and pure athletic ability. Those things help, of course, but only to a point. To tell the truth, I don't know if a strong-armed guy could ever play for us. They tend to be the guys who want to throw bullets, who want to put the ball through an earhole, who want to make quarterbacking into something macho. That's well and fine, but what we need are people who understand how to dump it off, who will look for someone to receive an underneath curl and be willing to make that pass instead of trying to thread the needle between two defensive backs twenty yards downfield. A lot of quarterbacks just can't resist the needle-threading challenge. It takes a lot more discipline than it does arm strength to play quarterback at BYU.

A great deal of the quarterback's job is anticipation. If there's anything the quarterback absolutely has to do at BYU, it's make the right decision; and he has to make it at the right time. *When* to throw is every bit as important as *where*. That's what makes it all go. Correct anticipation. Marc Wilson was a great anticipator, for example. He was smart and accurate, and he read defenses as well as anyone. He had a great feel. He got the ball to the right people at the right time. He didn't hold on to the ball too long, but he did hold on to it long enough. Unfortunately, in the pros he was drafted by the Raiders, and in my opinion that wasn't the right system for him. Everything the Raiders did was vertical. Their forte was the long routes. All of a sudden he was in a system where you didn't throw the ball until your receiver made his break. He'd been taught to anticipate, and now they were requiring him to react.

The quarterbacks who have thrived at BYU have all had great understanding. That understanding, that feel, is an innate thing, something I think you either have or you don't. You can't really coach it. If you don't have it, you can become an adequate quarterback, and probably a pretty good one in the right system. If you do have it, you can really do things in a system that calls for those kinds of skills.

For all their contrasting styles, that innate ability to understand has been the common quality shared by Gary Sheide, Gifford Nielsen, Marc Wilson, Jim McMahon, Steve Young, Robbie Bosco, Steve Lindsley, Bob Jensen, Sean Covey, Ty Detmer, Ryan Hancock, and John Walsh—all the regulars who have played on our system at BYU. In some cases they were not necessarily the most athletic quarterbacks on the team, or the fastest, and in most cases they weren't the ones with the strongest arms. But they always knew what they were looking for and they kept their heads when they needed to.

People often ask me to explain the genesis of the kind of passing game that's evolved at BYU. Where exactly did it come from? The answer is, I'm not sure—but I do know it didn't come from the mind of an old single-wing coach who grew up in Orem. I do know that a lot of what Doug Scovil developed here was the same as what Bill Walsh was developing at the time with the Cincinnati Bengals (where one of his quarterbacks, briefly, was Dewey Warren) and then at Stanford and San Diego before he went to the 49ers. Doug and Bill didn't ever coach together, but they knew each other, and they were obviously students of the same school of passing—utilizing the backs, utilizing the tight end, getting the ball off quickly, all of that.

What Bill went on to use to win three Super Bowls with the San Francisco 49ers was very similar to what Doug got us doing at BYU. The motions and the formations weren't identical, and the numbering systems were different, but the plays and concepts were basically the same. I found it interesting that when Mike Holmgren went to San Francisco from our staff, the 49ers started using the tight end even more often, more like what we'd been doing. Whether they were borrowing our ideas or not, I'm not sure, but there's no question the BYU and 49er systems were compatible, and still are, for that matter.

We weren't going to be able to hang on to Doug Scovil forever. He actually left BYU twice. The first time was after the 1977 season, when he went to the Chicago Bears. After just one season, he returned, staying until after the 1980 season, when he became the head coach at San Diego State University. The season between his two terms with us, in 1978, proved to be the most tumultuous of my coaching career. That was the year we wound up alternating Jim McMahon and Marc Wilson at quarterback, because of injuries. That situation, together with a new quarterback coach, Wally English, who took us away from many of the things we'd been doing, made for more turmoil than I thought was necessary. That year was good in that it made me determined to never again alternate quarterbacks and to not get away from the basic passing system we'd already established.

I've been fortunate to have some of the best coaches in the game work within that system. When Doug left, Ted Tollner came to us from San Diego State. When Ted was hired to be the head coach at USC we got Mike Holmgren, who later moved on to be the offensive coordinator for the San Francisco 49ers and then the head coach for the Green Bay Packers. Norm Chow took over the quarterback coaching responsibilities after Mike left, and Roger French became the offensive coordinator; later on we were able to bring in Robbie Bosco to coach the quarterbacks.

All of these coaches have built on and added to the basic concept first put to paper by Dewey Warren in 1972, with a major revision by Doug Scovil in 1976. There have been a lot of subtle changes since, but no significant departures from the blueprint.

Looking back on a relationship with the pass that's well into its third decade, I'm pleased that we've stayed loyal to our original basic concept. Over the years a lot of teams have used the passing game as a way to get out of hard times. But once they've put themselves back on track, they've returned to a more traditional run-oriented offense. At BYU I didn't want us to do that, and I'm satisfied that I can say we haven't. The passing game has been very, very good to BYU football, and I'd say BYU football has been very, very good to the passing game.

◁ *Posing with Lincoln High teammates Glenn Aiken, Leo Ferguson, and Ralph Willet in 1947. I'm on the right.*

▽ *After we won the state championship in 1948, we took Coach Sanky Dixon for a ride.*

△ *The Lincoln High track team. I'm in the front row, fourth from the left.*

▽ *Passing off as a Lincoln High Tiger.*

◁ *With Dad and Lewis, taking a break from milking those cows.*

▽ *(Left) Picture day as a Utah State Aggie.*

▽ *(Right) My official U.S. Army portrait.*

▷ *My wife, Patti.*

▽ *Four generations
of Edwards men:
LaVell, Matthew,
John, and Philo.*

◁ *Surrounded by four major reasons I've stayed employed. Going clockwise from the left, Gifford Nielsen, Marc Wilson, Ty Detmer, and Robbie Bosco.*

▷ *Two old coaches— Sanky Dixon and me.*

◁ *The Edwards family, all grown up. On the top row (left to right) there's LaMar, Don, Ruby, Max, Melba, Colleen, Norma, and Lewis; on the bottom row, I'm on the left, next to Alene, Ray, mother and dad, Shirley, and Wayne.*

▷ *Pat's folks, Louise and Irwin Covey, with two of the grandkids, Annie and Matthew.*

▽ *At the 1988 American Football Coaches Association convention in Atlanta. As the outgoing president, I'm giving the gavel to Joe Restic of Harvard, the incoming president. I'm the one smiling.*

◁ *Our family at Christmas. Pat and I are in the back. Clockwise from Pat there's Kelli, Lorri, Jim, John, Annie, Becky, Matthew, Ann, Ken, Dylan, Alec, and Philip.*

▷ *Florida State's Bobby Bowden, Mickey Mouse, and me. We were smart. We went to Disneyland before the game.*

◁ *Coaching at the East-West Shrine game in San Francisco with Ted Tollner and Jim Wacker (far right).*

◁ *The BYU staff in 1975. On the back row (left to right) there's Dwain Painter, Mel Olson, Fred Whittingham, Tom Ramage, Norm Chow, and Garth Hall. On the front row, Dick Felt is on my left and Dave Kragthorpe is on my right. I still know where all these guys are, but I don't know what happened to the shorts.*

◁ *With LDS Church President Spencer W. Kimball and BYU President Dallin H. Oaks.*

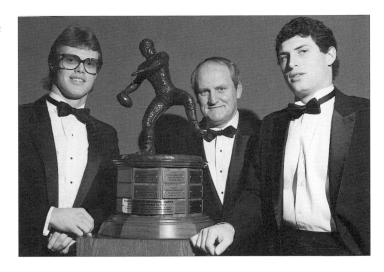

△ *At the Davey O'Brien quarterback awards ceremony with Jim McMahon and Steve Young. Two of the three of us would go on to win Super Bowls.*

◁ *Win a national championship, and your senator (Orrin Hatch) will take you to meet your president (Ronald Reagan).*

▽ *Team prayer.*

▷ *Laughing with Steve Young.*

▷ *Enjoying a trophy ceremony with WAC commissioner Joe Kearney.*
(Photography by Mark A. Philbrick)

◁ *There's nothing like winning a bowl game, especially when you haven't won one in a while. This is after getting past Oklahoma in the 1994 Copper Bowl.*
(Photography by David Sanders, *The Arizona Daily Star*)

△ *At a charity function with some of my favorite coaching friends. On the back row (left to right) there's Fred Whittingham, Dick Tomey, Jim Sweeney, and Ted Tollner. On the front row, I'm flanked by Dave Kragthorpe and Bill Yeoman.*

**Frown shots
through the years.**

The sideline yawn.
(Photography by
Don Grayston)

*The never-let-them-
see-you-sweat frown.*
(Photography by
Mark A. Philbrick)

*The all-purpose
frown.*

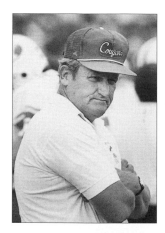

*The "I'm thinking"
frown.*

The pensive frown.

*The third-and-short
frown.*

△ *I've always gotten along with Utah's coaches. Here I'm getting a lift from Jim Fassel.*

△ *Getting a ride after win Number 200 in 1994.*

▽ *The chill of victory.*

△ *Waiting to tee off*
at the shrine itself:
Augusta National.

▽ *The bad news is*
I'm in the rough.
The good news
is the rough is
in Scotland.

▽ *You can't take*
the farm out of
the farmer.

The Chance

Chuck Cutler,
record-setting BYU receiver

The first time Chuck Cutler heard his head coach speak he was not impressed. Same with the second time, and the third time.

First time: "I'd just joined the BYU football team as a walk-on," says Cutler, "and this was the team meeting at the opening of camp. I'd heard about this man most of my life, one of the greatest, most successful coaches in the country. I'm thinking, 'Wow, I'm here. I'm a part of all this.' Then LaVell stood up and gave this little speech about not doing drugs and going to class. Then he sat down. 'Don't do drugs and go to class.' That was it."

Second time: "It was my first practice. The first time I saw LaVell all afternoon was when he gathered us together at the end and told us that was a fine practice. I found myself thinking, 'How does he know?'"

Third time: "I caught a little hitch pass in practice and turned to run. I was on the scout team, but I was acting like I was Jerry Rice, doing all this dancing, and I really got killed. As I was getting tackled, the ring finger on my left hand got caught in someone's face mask and was dislocated. I was in pain, rolling around on the ground. The trainers ran out, followed by LaVell. As they were popping my finger back into place, he looked down and said, 'Hey, Chuck, the next time you catch the ball, make one move, then run upfield.' That was it. Not 'How are you?' Or, 'Are you hurt?' Just, 'Make one move, then run upfield.' One thing I can say is I've never forgotten it. He doesn't do a lot of coaching, but give him credit for teaching at the appropriate time."

The fourth time Chuck Cutler heard his head coach speak, however, he *was* impressed.

"Between my sophomore and junior years he pulled me aside and told me that out of the group of receivers I was a part of, one of us would surface to be our next wide receiver," says Cutler. "That's how he put it, 'our next wide receiver.' I knew what he meant by that. He was referring to the line of great wide receivers they'd had at BYU through the years. He just matter-of-factly said, 'It's up to you to decide whether the next one is you or someone else—but someone will surface.'"

Cutler took the cue. He felt confident that if he worked hard he'd get his chance. What had happened to other walk-ons could happen to him. Humble beginnings didn't have anything to do with it, and it was a good thing because beginnings didn't get much more humble than his. The first time he went to the equipment room for cleats they told him he couldn't have any. He'd had to call coach Norm Chow to intervene, and then he got used cleats. "Talk about sitting in the back of the bus," says Cutler. "I think that will be the last phase in the equality thing. They'll recognize walk-ons."

BYU never did time him in running the forty. "They didn't want to know and neither did

I," he says. But they never barred him from the practice field, either.

That, and the fact that he was confident he "could catch the ball" is what kept him playing. That's what got him to come to BYU after a year of junior college football in the first place. Word gets around. This was a place for guys like him, a place where size and speed weren't the only prerequisites. "I was a scrawny slow guy from Draper, Utah," says Cutler. "And they said that was okay. They said that by and large, the program was fueled by guys like me."

He was redshirted in 1985 and was only slightly less invisible as a sophomore in 1986 when he played on the scout squad. But as a junior, as advertised, he got his chance—and he made the most of it. By his senior year he was teaming with Ty Detmer to lead the team with sixty-four receptions, ten for touchdowns. Eight of them came in eight straight games to tie an NCAA record for touchdown passes in consecutive games.

Cutler was mentioned on a number of All-America teams at the end of his senior season and was courted by the NFL. For a variety of reasons, among them multiple surgeries he'd had on his hands, he told the pros he wasn't interested. He didn't let them time him, either.

"I'd see LaVell," says Cutler, "and he'd roll his eyes and say, 'The pro scouts keep asking me if you have a drug problem. I tell them, "He doesn't even drink coffee. He's just an oddball kid who doesn't want to play pro football."'"

Cutler laughs. "I always got to make my own

decisions," he says. "Even at the end, when I decided not to try pro ball, LaVell didn't intervene, like most coaches might. He didn't try to talk me into it one way or the other. I always felt like I was free to go where I wanted to go, not where somebody else wanted me to go. Looking back on it, the thing I appreciate most is just getting the opportunity to try, to see how far I could go. That's what LaVell Edwards gave me. He gave me the chance."

CHAPTER FIVE

Philosophy

I came about my football philosophy the old-fashioned way: I let others beat it into me.

I'm sure I'm not alone in that regard. In one way or another, every coach is going to form his attitudes about the game based even more on his frustrations than on his successes. Through defeat comes resolve—resolve that if you can help it, you'll never go through that again.

One of my earliest "learning experiences" came in high school when we found ourselves with a first down next to the goal line at the end of the game. A touchdown meant we'd win the game. It was that simple. And so were we. We took four cracks at it, straight on, up the middle, and never made it.

It wasn't so much not scoring the touchdown that bothered me. I'd been on the other side enough to appreciate good defense. What bothered me, and I mean really nagged at me, was that we didn't have any options in that situation other than trying to power the ball across the goal line.

That frustration stayed with me. Objectively, I knew we weren't as strong as the team we were going up against, and when that happens, nine times out of ten you'll lose when you go head to head. When you're not the strongest team on the field, you need alternatives. I knew we were limiting ourselves without more creativity.

It was that kind of thinking that ultimately had a lot to do with the direction we would later go at BYU, both offensively and defensively. I wanted to have a playbook with enough options in it to be able to respond—hopefully with success—to whatever we ran up against. (At the same time, I've never wanted to be radical or flamboyant just for the sake of being radical or flamboyant.) If I was inherently conservative, that was fine. But I wanted to be conservative with a lot of bullets. If we were limited to some extent by our personnel, I didn't want that to mean we couldn't still win.

In a nutshell, that's the foundation of my basic football philosophy. My personal game plan was born out of searching for ways to make the playing field level. I don't ever want to have to concede defeat because the opposition might be bigger, faster, stronger, or all three.

Usually, they have been.

For the sake of simplicity, it would be fair to say that when it became obvious that a power dive up the middle just wasn't going to cut it, the forward pass eventually became the "option" I was looking for.

For any coach starting out, the game plan is where it begins. When you're young you formulate one, and over the years—hopefully you'll get enough of them—you refine it. Each coach develops his own game plan, and none is exactly like the others. They're like fingerprints or DNA. There are as many game plans as there are coaches.

In the beginning, a head coach will typically adopt a game plan similar to those he's had experience with as a player and assistant coach. But even at that, it's going to be different. Over time, probably quite a bit different. That's why none of Vince Lombardi's assistant coaches became Vince Lombardi when they became head coaches. No matter how hard they tried. Only Vince Lombardi could be Vince Lombardi.

And even that took a while. Developing into a coach requires time; it requires starts and stops and plenty of trial and error. For every coach you see who starts out with one approach and stays there, there are going to be at least five hundred who don't. You might think you have all the answers in the beginning, but you soon realize that you don't even know all the questions.

Putting a game plan in place and establishing a program that will execute it calls for as much inventiveness as you can manage—and then some. The landscape is always changing. Your personnel are always changing, your staff is always changing, your opponents are always changing—and the game itself is constantly evolving. You need to respond to all of it.

You're finished before you begin if you're always changing too.

Not in all areas, of course. You have to adapt to new players, new offensive and defensive techniques, rules changes, and so on. But to your basic game plan and your basic program—once they're established—you have to stay true. If it's working, don't fix it, and don't trade it in on a newer model.

Looking back on the way my coaching career evolved, I can see how fortunate I was to know by the time I became a collegiate head coach that whatever system I put into place, I needed to stick to it. The system in place at BYU in the '90s—and by now it seems to run almost by auto pilot—isn't appreciably different from the one we first established in the '70s. Its boundaries have become inherently understood.

In a nutshell, my football philosophy is based primarily on the following tenets.

LOYALTY WILL GET YOU . . . LOYALTY

Probably the most prevalent second-guessing of BYU football questions our tendency to play our older, more experienced players. Anyone even casually familiar with our program knows that the typical BYU lineup contains predominantly upperclassmen.

Quite often we'll bring in a heralded recruit with all kinds of credentials and press clippings, and then when he spends his first couple of years backing up an upperclassman, people will wonder why the player isn't playing more, if not starting. If he's such a superstar, what's he doing on the bench?

I think that's a perfectly understandable thing for fans to wonder about. For one thing, that isn't necessarily the way it would be anywhere else, and for another, new recruits do get considerable publicity. It's only natural to eagerly anticipate their contributions.

But our objective has never been to build a program that's based on individual talent as much as it's based on the belief that the team as a whole needs to be talented. And that can only happen when the players on the team learn a system that takes time—and often a lot of it—to really be understood.

When players come into the program and have the time to look at what the players ahead of them are doing—how they're concentrating, how much they're into it—that can be a big help. A lot can be learned by watching. Once a player buys into what we do, then he's in a position to really contribute.

As a player pays his "dues," it's also going to dawn on him that he's in a program that's going to give him his turn—because he's seen that it gives everyone a turn. If he sticks with it, he's going to have a chance.

We keep a lot of players who shouldn't be on the team—not if you look at their ability level starting out. But it's amazing what can happen when a player is given enough time to make mistakes and develop. Over time, we've realized a high ratio of success with players who have the discipline and the patience to stick with the system.

Any number of players have gone from the scout (or preparation) team to the starting team after they've had sufficient time to prepare. We've had a lot of those kinds of players over the years—overnight sensations who enrolled five or six years before. Otis Sterling is a good example. He was around the program for years without a scholarship. He was a senior before he ever had any grant-in-aid, and he was in law school before he ever started a game as a receiver. But he had a great attitude and he stuck with it; and before he was through he was successful by everyone's standards, his and the program's.

Some years we've had as many as half a dozen fifth-year seniors starting for us who have hardly played before. Some of our very best players over the years, in terms of honors, haven't started, or played very much at all, until their junior or senior seasons. In the case of returned missionaries, they often may not start until five or six years after they first arrive as freshmen. Many of our top receivers, in particular, have spent plenty of time being anonymous, players such as Chuck Cutler, Andy Boyce, David Mills, and Scott Phillips, to name a few.

Of course, this holds especially true when it comes to the quarterback position. With only a few exceptions, any quarterback who has started for us has gone through an apprentice period. He's worked his way up through the system. For a long stretch of time we never had a quarterback who started for us for more than two seasons—and almost every quarterback during that stretch was an All-American. The time Steve Young spent backing up Jim McMahon wasn't wasted time at all. In its own way it was as valuable as his playing time. The same went for the two years Robbie Bosco spent behind Steve Young, and so on.

At all positions, seeing the players ahead of you go through the steps makes it easier for you to go through those same steps. You'll be willing to work on the scout team for a year when you know that Ty Detmer did the same thing. You'll serve your time as a backup to an upperclassman. Then you'll get your shot. That's the program. If you stick with it, you'll appreciate it so much more when it's your turn.

This isn't always the case, of course. We've had freshmen and sophomores play for us, and some have made great contributions. And there are always going to be injuries and transfers to deal with. But for a younger player to start ahead of an older player at BYU, he can't just have equal ability, or even slightly better ability. He has to have considerably more ability.

It can take a while for all this to sink in for a new player. We'll have freshmen who look at the senior they're playing behind and think, "I'm faster than he is, and I'm younger, so why don't they use me instead of some guy who's going to be all washed up at the end of the season?" They'll invariably have roommates and friends who agree with them and get them even more worked up. They'll hear, "Yeah, you *are* better than that guy."

But then what happens the next year, or the year after that, when a new all-star comes in and, using the same reasoning, wants to take *that* player's job?

It's a vicious cycle that can have you constantly operating from the bottom instead of the top. You'll always be building for the future, always going for the quick fix, always developing, instead of taking advantage of what you've built. So many times I've seen football coaches, particularly in high school, go with "youth movements." They'll scrap all their seniors and play their sophomores, building toward when those sophomores will be seniors. But what usually happens is that particular senior class doesn't pan out as well as they thought it would, and then where are they? They're back to using their sophomores again. And along the way they haven't instilled confidence in their program. Their players aren't going to feel any assurance at all that if they come to practice and work hard, it will translate into getting a legitimate chance to play.

When a player knows he'll have a chance—a real chance—if he'll just hang in there, it only follows that he'll develop better patience. He'll be content to hang in there. We've found this is particularly true for outgoing missionaries. If a missionary knows he's going to have his position back when he returns, or at least that he'll be given every benefit of the doubt, then he's going to be willing to take the time to get ready to play again upon his return. Even though he's taken two years off and his physical conditioning is going to take some effort, he'll be mentally willing to paying the price. Players will work and stay loyal to a program that stays loyal to them.

HEY, IT'S NOT MY TEAM . . .

I have never felt that it's conducive to a team concept to operate as a head coach under the assumption that the wins are *my* wins, that the losses are *my* losses, and, in general, that it's *my* team. Sooner or later, the players are going to realize that it's them doing all the hitting and the sweating. It's them trying to stop the tailback and run a crossing pattern against double coverage. They're the ones who are making it happen, or not happen.

It's the players' team. It isn't my team. Every year at the start of August workouts I make a point of telling our players just that: "This is your team. It's up to you to decide what you want to make of it. What happens this season, especially for you seniors, is something you'll take with you the rest of your life. Remember that and make it a season you'll be proud of.

"I'll be back next year," I always remind them.

If the players don't determine for themselves that they're going to work hard to be successful, if what they're doing isn't *their* idea, rather than the coaches', then when things don't go well, it's easy for it to be somebody else's fault. It makes it easy to shift the blame. It's not hard to relinquish ownership for something you didn't feel was yours in the first place.

Another thing about that welcoming speech. I make it a point to talk about the importance of being prepared. In fact, I talk about the importance of being prepared anytime I have the chance. To me, preparation is what success always hinges on. Emotion doesn't get you very far, and neither does a lot of talk. But preparation does. If you prepare yourself for whatever opportunities might present themselves during the season, then you're going to be successful. It's the players who work hard during the off season (lifting weights and running and practicing their position skills) who find themselves in the middle of success once the season gets underway.

The preparation is theirs, too, not mine. It's when a player takes responsibility for his own progress and looks on the team as being "his" team—feeling he has as much ownership of it as anyone—that he opens the door to opportunity and sets himself, and his team, up for success.

THERE ARE WORSE THINGS TO BE CALLED THAN FUNDAMENTALLY SOUND

If no one else, I know I've pleased my high school football coach, Sanky Dixon, by stressing fundamentals. At Lincoln High School we never held a practice without spending time on the basics. At BYU, same story. If our players want to blame anyone, they can blame Sanky.

Football is hard enough without trying to skip the basics. More than perhaps any other team sport, football demands practice. No matter what offense you're running, or what defense, you have to go over what you're doing again and again and again. Teamwork comes only after repetitions, and then more repetitions. Virtually no other sport has a practice-to-playing ratio like football. Even the pros practice all week for a single game.

Every practice session is one more opportunity to get better at what you're trying to do. Pass blocking is always going to be pass blocking. A 66—that's one of our passing plays—is always going to be a 66. The idea is to become so efficient that during a game—when everything seems to go at hyperspeed, when the stands are full, when the game is on the line—your reactions will be pure reflex. That efficiency will kick in. Practice is the time to understand what's going on, to study, to let it all sink in.

Practice is not about winning and losing, and it's not about showing off. When we practice passing drills, for instance, we tell the scout team that their job isn't to take out any receivers or beat the offense, but it's to give the offense the kind of opposition it's going to get from whoever we might be playing that week. In practice, we need to see what we're going to see on Saturday.

A good practice player, one who is paying attention and trying to always learn something new, will see it pay off in the games. Jim McMahon was an excellent example of that. If something went wrong on a play we were running in practice, if there was some kind of a mix-up, he was the kind who would stop and ask questions. He wanted to know why this player was here and why that player was there. He was always questioning. Always learning.

Practicing fundamentals can get routine or even downright boring. I know that. But there's no substitute for it. Through firsthand experience I've seen that it works. Time after time, season after season, the players and teams that are having success are the ones that are fundamentally sound. They're not necessarily the most talented teams. There have been years when we've won eight or nine games and we haven't had an All-American quarterback, or any other All-Americans. We've actually never relied all that much on talent. We haven't had that luxury. If we went by the lists that rate the top recruiting classes in the country, we'd quit right there. We've never been listed among those schools that have signed the top high school graduates. We've never put a lot of guys in the pros. What we have relied on are good, hardworking kids who execute and practice as hard as they play.

When Ted Tollner first came to BYU as an assistant coach—he'd come from San Diego State, where he'd coached against us for a number of years—he walked off the field after his first practice with us and said, "Are you telling me that these are the kind of people you've been winning the league with all these years?"

Ted was used to coaching speed, and he didn't see much speed, and he wasn't overwhelmed by our level of talent. On the surface, he couldn't see anything in Provo he hadn't seen anywhere else. Even if it was backhanded, I took it as one of the best compliments the program has ever had.

WIN OR LOSE, MONDAY IS ALWAYS GOING TO BE . . . MONDAY

Whether we win on Saturday by a hundred or lose by a hundred, we're back out on the field Monday for our regular practice. Rain or shine, it's business as usual. There is very little deviation—and none that's based on whether we won or lost.

I've never brought a team back on Monday after a big loss and said, "Okay, we're going to find out who wants to play" or "We're going back to double sessions until we get this worked out." I've also never brought a team back after a big win and given them the day off. We'll talk about what happened in our last game, of course. We want to learn from it, whatever it was. But we don't want to go so far that we confuse *last* Saturday with *this* Saturday. The idea is to prepare for the future instead of reacting to the past.

I can get frustrated after a loss and feel as bad as anyone. But it doesn't mean I'm going to change or allow frustration to affect my decision making or our usual schedule.

A football team needs consistency, and it's hard to have consistency on a roller coaster. Week in, week out we run the same kinds of practices. Win, lose, or draw, we keep to our schedule. We don't put the pads on for Monday's practice. On Tuesday and Wednesday we go full pads. On Thursday we go shoulder pads and shorts, and on Friday we walk through for our game preparation. That's our schedule and we stick to it.

At BYU we've had a history of playing well at the end of the season.

I think that's a reflection of our steady approach. Too much wear and tear, either physical or emotional, can have you worn down by the time November comes along.

COACHES GET TIRED OF PLAYERS, TOO

At a private religious school like BYU, where Sunday practice has always been against institutional policy, we've always given the players—and the coaches—that day off. Over time I've come to appreciate the value of that day away from football. The players need a day away from the coach, and the coach needs a day away from the players. And beyond that, it gives everyone a chance to relax, to take a deep breath, and to get recharged.

If I were to coach anywhere else I'd still want to make sure we took a day off every week. The season is long enough and hard enough as it is without making it seem like one long, continuous week.

THERE IS AN "I" IN TEAM

Football may be the ultimate team game, but a good team will also be constantly aware of the individual. Unnecessary stifling of individual skills and creativity only stifles team skills and creativity. We try to stress individuality by not trying to fit everyone into the same mold. We don't want our players to talk the same, walk the same, or play the same. Ideally, what the team does should reflect the player's individual strengths.

The quarterbacks who have played at BYU perhaps best reflect that penchant for individuality. We've had a tremendous variety of personalities and playing styles at that position. If we'd locked in to one style of player, and one personality type, I'm sure we wouldn't have had the same results. Luckily, we were able to adapt. We were able to use Marc Wilson one year and Jim McMahon the next, for example, and allow each to work within the framework of his personality and what he did best.

Included on the list of All-Americans we've had at quarterback are extroverts, introverts, and everything in between. We've had guys who didn't want to talk to the media and guys who did. We've had guys who screamed and guys who never raised their voices. We've had tall guys; we've had short guys. As for playing style, we've run the spectrum from scramblers to guys who never wanted to leave the pocket. It's true, they've all worked within our basic framework. But beyond that they've all played their own style. They've been allowed to compete with what they do best, physically and emotionally. If we'd been too rigid along the way, I don't think it would have ever worked.

That's where the feel comes in. As a coach, I think you have to have that feel every bit as much as a quarterback does. You have to sense things; you have to know your players. You have to know what they'll do (and just as important, what they're capable of doing). One night I was watching a replay of the 1984 Holiday Bowl game against Michigan. That was the game when Robbie Bosco came back from the training room and led us on those two fourth-quarter drives that won the game and allowed us to win the national championship. Here's a guy who, when he was off the field, didn't even like to get up and speak; you had to practically drag him into press conferences. His nature was introverted and shy. And yet put him on the field and put his back against the wall, and there's no way you were going to hold him back. What causes people to do that? Where does that kind of competitiveness come from? That ability to go to another level? I'm not sure. I really don't know. So many times, I've sat back and been amazed by the things players do.

As much as anything, I think what coaching really comes down to is putting the right people in the right places, providing them with a decent game plan, and letting them run it. When Joseph Smith said, "Teach them correct principles and let them govern themselves," he could easily have been talking about football coaching. Once you've taught them the principles, be smart and get out of their way.

Dick Tomey,
former University of Hawaii
coach, currently coaching at
University of Arizona

Putting with the Enemy

Enough time has elapsed. Probably. Although you never know. There might still be a University of Hawaii alumnus out there who's going to hear this and cancel his contributions check.

But Dick Tomey is willing to give it a chance. This is the best example he's got of his friend LaVell Edwards being an unusual man to coach against. And besides, Tomey's no longer at the University of Hawaii anyway.

"We used to play golf," says Tomey. "Friday morning. Seven A.M. Waialae Country Club."

On the surface, no big deal.

Then Tomey adds, "The day before the football game.

"How many other coaches would I do that with?" Tomey continues. "Probably none."

This was in the '80s, when Tomey was the head football coach at the University of Hawaii and Edwards was the head football coach at Brigham Young. Most of the games between the Rainbow Warriors and the Cougars were played in Honolulu, and almost all of them were preceded by a game of golf between the two head coaches, played the day before the football game.

Clandestine golf.

Top-secret golf.

"We were sworn to secrecy," says Tomey. "Our golf didn't have an effect on the game and we both knew that, but still, it's not the kind of thing you want to publicize. The alumni would have had a field day.

"We really didn't worry about the media seeing us. We knew they were all sleeping in.

"We enjoyed playing golf together and we didn't have all that many opportunities, so we'd just get up early on Friday and play nine holes," Tomey explains. "I'd usually win the golf game, and then the next night he'd win the football game. If I'd had my choice, that's not exactly the pattern I'd have chosen."

For the record, Edwards' Cougars never did lose to Tomey's Warriors in the '80s. The coaches played against each other eight times and BYU won every game, six of them in the islands.

"The aggravating part was that the games were always so close," says Tomey. "This was when BYU was dominant. I mean really dominant. They'd win almost every WAC game they played. We were probably the most consistently competitive team against them. We had some great games, unbelievable games. But they won them all."

In five straight contests in Honolulu from 1984 through 1988, four of the five games were decided by a touchdown or less. From 1986 through 1988, the scores were 10–3, 16–14, and 24–23. Three losses by a grand total of ten points. BYU was as popular in Oahu as a tsunami. The Cougars needed a police escort just to make it to the airport.

Still, the coaches remained friends. Their

Friday morning tee times were never canceled. Never came close.

"I disliked BYU. I disliked BYU a lot," says Tomey, who moved on to the University of Arizona in 1989. "On my list of those I really wanted to beat, there was no one higher.

"But that didn't transfer over to how I felt personally about LaVell Edwards. I was able to separate the game competition from our personal association, and so was he. We became better friends over the seasons, not worse. We could play golf on Friday morning and then really go after each other on the football field Saturday night. I'm not just saying that. It was honestly no problem for either one of us.

"I have to admit, with most people I just wouldn't feel comfortable doing that," says Tomey. "With most people, that wouldn't work. With LaVell it did. After I went to Arizona I missed that. I've been trying to get him back on the schedule ever since."

If there's one thing I'm sure about it's this: I will not go down in history as a hands-on football coach. Those coaches who move players out of the way and proceed to give a personal demonstration of how to hit the blocking sled? Who tell the assistant coach in charge of the linebackers to step aside for a minute so they can take over? That's not me.

I was like that when I was a high school coach, of course. Like most high school coaches, I did just about everything but cut the grass. I'd hit the sled. I'd demonstrate the three-point stance. And as an assistant coach in college I continued to get down in the trenches, as they say. But as a head coach I have been just about as invisible as you can possibly be. This is not by accident. It is by design. I like it that way. I want it that way.

And let me add right here that it's not as easy as it looks.

It's hard to go to the practice field every day and just stand around. I'm on my feet all day. My legs are killing me. My hips are sore. I'm watching the same drills I've watched a thousand times before. Practice is ten times longer for me than it is for anyone else. Sometimes I look for people to talk to. The invention of the cellular phone has been a big blessing for me.

But as far as I'm concerned, all this comes with the job description. As the head coach, I see my job at practice—and in games, too, to a large extent—to primarily be an observer, an overseer. The position coaches coach the positions, the players play, and I stand around and . . . manage.

Management has its moments of involve-

CHAPTER SIX

Management

ment, of course. There are times in practice when I'll purposely raise my voice, sometimes just to get a rise out of someone, just to maintain control, to let them know I'm there. And there are decisions, in practice and in games, that are the head coach's and the head coach's alone. Game decisions such as: Do we go for it on fourth down? Do we kick the field goal? Do we try for one point or two? Practice week decisions such as: Do we play zone or man? What packages do we want to use against the rush? Ultimately, the final say is up to the head coach.

DELEGATE AND GET OUT OF THE WAY

I've never had a problem making those kinds of decisions, just as I've never had a problem getting out of the way once they've been made. I prefer to manage that way. To me that's what managing is: Put things in their place and then let them function. That goes for everything—for the game plan, for the players, for the coaches, for the equipment men, you name it. Once an area of responsibility has been established, give it room to work.

Where does this management philosophy come from? A lot of it probably goes back to watching my dad when I was growing up on the farm. Once he gave you a job he let you do it, and he let you keep doing it until you got it finished.

I know it goes back, too, to when I was an assistant coach at BYU to Tommy Hudspeth. He left the coaches alone and I liked that. He spent a little more time with the offense, because that's what he was more familiar with. But he basically told us that the defense—that's where I coached—was our area and he let us coach it. That had a big impact on me. I really appreciated the freedom to be able to coach. I appreciated not having everything I did under close scrutiny, always subject to change. For eight years I enjoyed that freedom. As the defensive coordinator I felt I was genuinely in charge, and that felt good to me. I know I was able to really develop as a coach that way.

When I became the head coach I was determined to give my assistant coaches that same kind of freedom. As much as possible, I would stay out of their way and let them coach. I've tried to never lose sight of that. It hasn't always been easy. The urge to meddle can be a strong one. In the early years, particularly, I had to fight the feeling that I should be more in the middle of what was going on.

I wore a headset during games for a while. I'd switch channels back and forth between the defense and the offense. But I came to the conclusion that I just didn't like it. I already knew what plays we were going to run. I knew what our game plan was. I knew what players we were going to play. If there were things I wanted changed, I'd have already discussed that with the staff during the week. We weren't going to change now, during the game. So why not let the coaches do their jobs, and why not give me the freedom to be able to think clearly about the decisions I would need to make during the game?

For me, what it's always come down to is this: If you're going to delegate, delegate.

There was one game, in particular, that brought this point home to me early in my BYU career. We were playing at Colorado State not long after I'd become head coach. I didn't know a lot about the passing game, which is why I'd gone out in the first place and found coaches who did. But during that game at Fort Collins I felt compelled, for some reason, to get involved with the instructions to the quarterback and the receivers. I felt, as the head coach, that maybe I was looking a little too out of it by just standing around with my hands in my pockets. Maybe I should appear more active, more involved. So I got in the middle of this discussion and that discussion, adding my two cents worth wherever I could.

No one said anything to me. No one said I was out of place or that I shouldn't be there. How could they? I was the head coach. But after the game I thought about it and decided that wasn't what I wanted to be doing. I knew I wasn't adding a whole lot, except to the confusion. The only thing I might have helped was my sideline image and I guess my ego—and not by much at that. So I "retired" as a meddler.

I'm sure if you asked any of the coaches who were there, they wouldn't even remember anything specific about that game, or that anything out of the ordinary went on. It was just one of those otherwise nondescript games that nonetheless had a profound impact on me and would help shape the way I would act and do things in the future. I don't believe I've worn a headset since.

It would be different if you were a one-man staff. But we've never been a one-man staff at BYU, and hopefully we never will be. I remember how important it was when we were able to expand the coaching staff so ours was as large as most of the schools we played. The value of a full-sized staff has never been lost on me. If you've got them, why not use them?

As the head coach you're in charge of that staff, of course. You should never lose sight of that. That's your job. It's your responsibility to keep it all together. You're the one who answers for the wins and the losses, for the bottom line. You're the one who fits all the different parts together. If that isn't full-time work, I don't know what is.

To me, effective head coaching doesn't begin with headsets; it begins with trust. It's trust that ties all the parts together. Developing trust is a two-way street. I don't think you generate real trust if you're constantly looking over the shoulder of the person you're supposed to be trusting. If an assistant coach has a responsibility, then let it truly be his responsibility. Trust him with it.

I've never believed in fear motivation, because it's not based on trust. It's based on being afraid of the consequences. Fear motivation does work for some people in the coaching business—and in other areas of management—and I'm sure that's fine for them. But my desire has always been to maintain an environment that is conducive to trying things without fear of failure. I think you still have to be tough and demanding. But demanding doesn't have to mean demeaning. Intimidation is not my nature anyway. I've given very few ultimatums in my life, and generally when I have they haven't been worth anything—because it's me that has always backed off.

I've never felt I have to go around and remind anybody that I'm the head coach, and I've often wondered at coaches who will do that. The very fact that you're the head coach gives you all the authority you need, sometimes *more* than you need. Just the fact that you're sitting in the chair is all you need. If you can see yourself in that light, then I think you have a chance to go about the business of managing your program instead of being constantly concerned about managing yourself.

It's not necessary that others always agree with you, either, for you to have that unquestioned authority, and neither do you have to always be right. I'm sure that over the years a number of my assistant coaches haven't liked a lot of the things I've done. I know that they constantly wonder to themselves, or to each other, why I don't do this another way, or why I don't change this or that. And that's fine with me. I wouldn't want it any other way. I want them to do their own thinking. I want them to have that leeway. I think it's healthy and I think it's their right. People have a right to question and a right, for that matter, to make mistakes. Myself included.

I know in my own mind when I've made a mistake or when I haven't used good judgment. I also know that the times I'm the most disappointed in myself is when I realize the reason I've used bad judgment is that I've yielded to some outside influence or pressure—when I've essentially allowed someone or something else to decide for me.

Whether it's running a football program, a corporation, or a political party—no matter what it is—the key to effective management is using all the input available to make sound judgments that are either going to solve, avoid, or, at the very least, defuse problems.

Most of the time that's not going to happen immediately.

Many times, a problem will come up and I have no clue what to do about it. In fact, I find that happens a lot. The last thing I want to do when that happens is make a snap decision. I need to think about it. I need to mull it over. I need to worry about it. And most of all, I need to maintain control while all this is going on.

Whenever possible, I'll keep the problem to myself. I'll purposely not talk it over with others, particularly those who have a tendency to want to keep talking about it until it's resolved. Some things just take time, and I've always had an ability to put things on hold until I can get around to dealing with them. I can put them in the back of my mind and keep them in some compartment back there. They'll gnaw at me but they're not in the forefront, getting in the way of other things that need to be taken care of first. When I have time, I'll think the problem through and decide what to do about it.

That's the way I am, and I have to manage that way. I have strong feelings about working within the framework of who you are. I've never felt like my way is necessarily the best way, but it has to be the best way for me.

HEALTHY DIVERSITY

One of me is plenty for my staff. If I met someone just like me, I wouldn't hire him. I've tried to always have a diverse coaching staff, with perspectives coming from a variety of directions. We've had a lot of continuity over the years, with very little staff turnover, but that doesn't mean it's always just one big happy family. I'm pleased to say that there's always been a certain amount of unrest and discord. There's always someone saying we ought to be doing something different. That's healthy. It's healthy to have variety; it's healthy to have a little disputing going on.

It's healthy, for example, to have a Roger French who's always stirring the pot. It's Roger's craziness that's kept things off balance for us, just a little bit, over the years. He'll keep guys on their toes, he'll get them mad or frustrated, yet they like him and they want to play for him. That's his personality and I think it's been very valuable to the staff. If we didn't have that with Roger, or with a Ken Schmidt, I'd have to try to do a little of that myself—which I've done over the years—but if they do it and if it's consistent with their personalities, it works so much better.

It's true, teams do tend to take on the personality of the coach, and it's always made a lot of sense to me to take advantage of the assets of every coach on the staff. That way a team can take on the personality that is a composite of the strengths of a number of personalities. And the head coach can be the composite of those strengths as well.

I always have relied on the strengths of others as much as my own. Over time, the benefits only increase. Our current staff serves as a good example of that. Norm Chow is our assistant head coach and play-caller, and you'd be hard pressed to find a better student of the game. Norm is like a sponge. He picks up everything he sees, and after all the time he's spent in the program that amounts to a lot. As a result he has a very good feel for calling a game. He makes sure we stay within our game plan. He's really the glue that keeps us together. Norm keeps us honest.

Roger French works with Norm to coordinate the offense, and also coaches the offensive line, and it doesn't take much time at all around Roger for either a player or a coach to see that he never stops coaching, not for a single down, whether it's spring ball or the middle of the season. He has a singleness of purpose that is remarkable.

Like Norm and Roger, Lance Reynolds, our offensive backfield coach, is an old offensive lineman—it seems like we're surrounded by offensive linemen—who has a great feel for the game. He brings a high level of intelligence and understanding to the staff. The same can be said of Robbie Bosco, our quarterback coach, who is developing into an excellent teacher. Robbie was the winningest quarterback we've had as a player, and he communicates that knack for winning as a coach.

Chris Pella handles our kickers and also coordinates our recruiting and does an excellent job in both areas. Chris was formerly a head coach at Utah State. He's great with people, a very popular coach who gives a lot of stability to the program.

Ken Schmidt, our defensive coordinator, came to BYU after winning titles everywhere he coached, at high school in Salt Lake City and in junior college at Ricks College. He adds an exceptionally high level of intensity to the program.

Tom Ramage, our defensive line coach, came to the staff the second year I was head coach. He's been as important as anyone at establishing the quiet confidence and expectations that have helped propel the program.

Our longtime defensive backfield coach, Dick Felt, retired following the 1993 season, leaving such a sizable hole to fill that we replaced him with *two* defensive backfield coaches, DeWayne Walker and Barry Lamb, both of whom came on board for the 1994 season and immediately contributed. As they have time to develop, their personalities will emerge more and more.

Each coach contributes so much to the overall program that it's hard for me to imagine not having their input. Chuck Stiggins, the only strength coach we've ever had at BYU, is an excellent example of someone whose value just keeps increasing. In the '70s he was the one who began educating all of us on the value of weight training. Over the years he's been a real student of effective weight training, and the benefits to the program have been invaluable.

I've always tried to have diversity on the staff. I've tried to have guys who are drivers. I've tried to have guys who are laid back. I've tried to have authoritarians. I've tried to have thinkers and tinkerers and therapists. My thinking is that if there's enough variety, things will stay churned up and we'll keep moving. You have to have that on a football staff. You can't have so much harmony that it puts you to sleep. You can't let familiarity take over, because familiarity will kill you.

That doesn't mean you want to work from a crisis mentality. The ultimate goal, of course, is to avoid crises, to manage what happens instead of having what happens manage you. The trick is to keep everything juggled so it all works together and doesn't pull itself apart. If you overreact or react early, you set yourself up for a never-ending series of big problems.

More often than not, I've found that time and clear thinking are a head coach's most valued assets. Without them, the volatile nature of a world as competitive as football can be reduced to just one headache after another. But usually when you mix time and rationality into a situation, you can defuse a problem and make it manageable. Situations that otherwise could rip apart your program can gradually disappear, leaving little residue.

As an illustration of that, let me tell you about an incident that happened early in the 1991 season. That was Ty Detmer's senior year, and to say the least, we didn't get off to a strong start. We lost to Florida State in the Disneyland Classic, then we lost at UCLA, and we followed that by getting beat up pretty good at Penn State. The curse of the Heisman got us, I guess. Before we knew it we were 0 and 3 and getting ready to play Air Force in Provo.

Needless to say, nerves were a bit frayed by this point. But the good news was, we hadn't played a league game yet. We were still undefeated in the WAC, and in Provo.

I knew that's what our focus needed to be when we returned from Penn State. But early in the practice week we had a major distraction when a fight broke out. Winless teams can get pretty frustrated, and I know frustration had a lot to do with these players going at it. Words were said and feelings got out of control. There were black and white players involved, and the problem included an element of racial taunting. The team just kind of froze when the fighting and yelling started.

Everyone was upset—the players, the coaches, me. I had to order the players involved off the practice field. I told them to wait by my office. One by one they came in and we talked about what happened. In the meantime, the debates had already begun out on the practice field. There were those who thought one player had instigated the fight and it was his fault. Others thought it was another player. There was some racial posturing going on.

I wasn't really sure what to do, but I knew what I didn't want to do. I didn't want to make a big issue out of the situation right then. I didn't want to make any threats or ultimatums. I wanted some time to think before I made any decisions.

I told the players that what they did wasn't right and to go home and think about it. I didn't sleep much that night, trying to decide what was the best thing to do. But as with most things, by the next afternoon's practice everyone's feelings were calmed down to the point where we could talk. The players were ready to make peace with each other, which they did, and when I talked to the team that day before practice I didn't even mention the incident. I talked about how we were still on track for our goal, to win the WAC, and we were all together in that.

I sensed that rather than standing up and making a big issue out of something that really could divide the team, I ought to just let it die. And it did. We had our best game of the year against Air Force that

Saturday, and we won seven of our last eight games that season. There were no more eruptions of that nature the rest of the year, and we did go on to win the league.

Not that the fight in practice was unusual. When you're involved in something as competitive as major college football, you're always going to have fights and other conflicts to deal with. And that's just the tip of the iceberg when it comes to being a head coach. It's amazing the things you have to concern yourself with.

THE GUY WITHOUT THE CLIPBOARD

So many different areas require your time and attention. You need to take time for the little lady who writes to you because she's concerned about something she saw or heard about one of your players. You need to take time for the bishop who calls about some other situation. You need to work with the media. You need to maintain good relationships with the administration, with the standards office, with security. You need to have time for the fans. That's one of the reasons I go on the radio for a call-in show after home games. We were a pioneer in that area, and I have to admit sometimes I wonder what we've created. But it's something that I think is valuable. And luckily, we've won most of our home games.

Gaining credibility—and good working relationships—in any of these areas of management takes effort. It can't just happen overnight, at BYU or anywhere else. That's what makes it difficult for a new coach. It takes time to establish how you're going to manage your program, how you're going to delegate, how you're going to handle all the various relationships. And you need to develop those relationships. Sometimes a new coach just doesn't get that time.

Perhaps the most valuable lesson I've learned when it comes to getting along with all the various groups a head coach needs to deal with—from the coaches on the staff to the professors on campus to the booster club and everything in between—is to listen. If you give people the chance to be heard, I've found that's often all that's needed. You may not agree with everything they're saying. Sometimes you may not agree with *anything* they're saying. But if you make them feel like they're having their chance to have their say, and you're giving it some genuine thought, the results are usually going to be quite positive. You've laid the groundwork toward a workable solution.

Several years ago, we had a relationship with BYU Security that wasn't at all healthy. A call from security would usually start out like this: "A bunch of your football players . . . "

As you might guess, that kind of approach didn't go over very well in the football office. Security's tendency to describe all the people in trouble as "football players" was purely an assumption. Usually, when everything got sorted out, other students would prove to be involved as well, and sometimes it would turn out that no football players were involved at all.

An adversarial relationship developed between the security department and the football department, and with every new "alleged" problem that adversarial relationship was perpetuated. One day I called the director of security and asked if I could visit with him. When we met I told him our concerns: that we felt football players were getting a bad rap in general and that we would appreciate it if they could be looked at simply as BYU students because that's what they were—students just like anyone else.

The director heard me out and responded positively to what I said. Then he talked about his frustrations. He said there was a feeling in his department that at the football office we weren't interested in hearing about any problems with our players, that we didn't want to discipline them. I assured him that was not the case. If we had players causing trouble, we wanted to know about it and we'd try to do something about it.

We've had an excellent relationship with security ever since that talk. Once we both established we were on the same side of the fence and we were both in the business of trying to help kids, the confrontational barriers came down. We both took the time to listen to each other.

I have never liked confrontation. I don't think it gets you anywhere.

And I've never felt a strong need to offer my opinion. If I have something to say I'll say it, but it's not important to me to get in the last word. I don't feel the need to do a lot of expounding. I'd rather keep something to myself and use it when it's going to serve a purpose. If, for instance, I see a coach on the staff doing something I don't agree with, I'll tell him about it. But I won't stop him in front of his players or in front of anybody else. I'll call him aside when it's possible and tell him what I'm thinking and see what we can work out.

Again, this is the way I'm made up, so it's the way I manage my program. Over the years I've found I'm effective only when I'm consistent with who I am. If I try to be somebody else it doesn't work very well. I could go out to practice, turn my hat around backwards, get out a big blow horn, and bark out instructions. I could stand on top of a tower. I could go through all the motions of "macho coaching." I could imitate other coaches. But none of that would be me. It would be me trying to be somebody else. And it wouldn't work.

Would the way I do things work for someone else? Not necessarily—I think everyone needs to find his or her own style. Because of the success we've had at BYU, I've had quite a few people study the way I do things. People from the business world have looked at the way I manage. They've wanted to know the secrets to how I delegate. People from other football programs have looked into what's behind our uncommon staff continuity, which is really quite unusual in a business that is primarily transient, and they've looked into what's behind a program over twenty years old that has never fired anyone.

In a lot of ways we have a program that is far from the norm. I'm aware of that. We're not all that conventional in general, and I'm not a conventional head coach. I know there are coaches and others who watch our practices and wonder what's going on. They wonder who the head coach is. They wonder what in the world I *do*.

Over the years I've thought about that, and how curious it must look. I'm the guy without the clipboard. I'm the guy over in the corner strolling, chewing his tongue. Who looks like he has all the time in the world.

A lot of it has to do with the fact that many of the things I do aren't visible. You can't see that I never stop listening or that I never stop fine tuning. I enjoy working behind the scenes. I get a lot of satisfaction from setting up the program and then watching it work.

If I do have a hidden ingredient, I suppose it's that I rely a great deal on feel. As a head coach I use feel—or intuition—to make many decisions. I think you probably have to have a kind of sixth sense to be an effective coach, as well as in most other leadership situations. You must learn to trust your own instincts.

Ultimately, I think management comes down to that. After all the computer printouts, after all the timing and the drills and the statistics, eventually you're going to have to plug in your intuition to complete whatever equation you're working on.

Where that feel comes from, I'm not certain. Experience enhances it, I'm sure, and being prepared helps, but there's an intangible involved too. It's very much like a quarterback when he comes to the line of scrimmage. He's got all these components at his disposal. He's got the coaches who have sent down his instructions from the press box. He's surrounded by players who will help him run the play; and when he comes up over his center and looks at the defense, he's got his training to know what might work and what might not. But should he run the play that was called from the press box, or should he audible to another play? What he decides to do is finally going to come down to what he has practiced and what his intuition tells him is the best call. It's the quarterback with a knack—who intuitively *knows* the right way to go—who finds success.

Managing a football program calls for essentially the same thing. What you don't consciously think about is as important as what you do. Maybe more so. When it works, you can't always say exactly why . . . but you're also not shocked that it did.

Down and Out . . . and Back

Glen Kozlowski looked in his rearview mirror and blinked—just to make sure he wasn't imagining all of this. He wasn't. That was Provo, Utah, all right, getting smaller by the second. What was going on, for crying out loud—that's what he wanted to know. He was supposed to be a big man *on* campus, not off it.

He'd made a mistake in his choice of a college, of that he was certain. He could have gone just about anywhere to school. They all wanted him. They all begged for him. He was All-Everything at Escondido High School. He could run, he could jump, he could catch the football with entire teams hanging onto his pads.

He'd certainly had better offers from other schools. Many schools had offered bonuses well beyond the basic tuition, books, and room and board. Something, you know, just between him and them. Something under the table. He chose BYU anyway. They threw the ball, and it made his mom happy.

Then they kicked him out.

He didn't even last a year. He was on the football team as a freshman, off to a promising start, when he got hurt halfway through the season. It was the first injury of his life and it stunned him. He'd suspected he might be immortal. To deal with the shock that he wasn't, he went to a few parties, did a few things he shouldn't have, things that weren't in line with the school's standards.

When they found out they sent him back to California. Officially he was on probation. He could come back if he shaped up.

Driving back toward the coast, two words stuck in his mind: Fat chance. The University of Miami had already been on the phone, and others would soon follow. The top programs still knew who he was, knew he was again available, and wouldn't treat him so shabbily.

"I wasn't going back," says Kozlowski now, a decade later, with a pro football career in the rearview mirror as well. "I wasn't going to let them push me around like that. I felt like I was a guy who had been wronged big time. I was bitter. It was like, 'Hey, wait a minute, you can't do this to me.'"

BYU's position had been simple enough. He had broken the rules, and he had to sit out a semester. Then he had to ask if he could come back. How about that for a switch? Him recruiting them.

"I was a punk," says Kozlowski. "No question about it. I came to BYU as a total punk kid. Then I got injured and I had to deal with that, which was a first for me. I didn't live by the rules. And because I was an athlete I thought it didn't matter. I thought they'd take care of me. For most athletes, your maturity level stops when you're sixteen years old because that's when people start taking care of you. But, if anything, it was just the opposite at BYU. If anything, because I was an athlete, it was harder. And deservedly so. I can say that now."

But not then.

Back home, Kozlowski got plenty of sympathy. He got plenty of encouragement to enroll someplace new, someplace that would treat him right.

But he also got something he didn't expect. He got encouragement from the very man who showed him the door.

"LaVell Edwards was the one who said I had to leave," says Kozlowski. "But he was also the one who said he wanted me to return.

"When I was back home in California, LaVell called from time to time," says Kozlowski. "He has this sense. He knows when to give you a call, and he knows when not to give you a call.

"After we'd talked a few times, and after enough time had passed, I realized I was dealing with an honest man who really did care about me as a person, not just as a football player. It was those talks with LaVell that made me face the fact that I had to grow up and take a stand. I could either change and be somebody I respected, or I could continue to be this little goof-off that I was. That's what it came down to.

"Fortunately, I had a coach who was willing to stay with me," Kozlowski continues. "LaVell has this ability to relate to the offbeat guys, to the guys who go with their own drummer. I think it's because he's like that too. He goes to his own drummer. He can put himself in your shoes and

walk with you. He understands people like me—
that can't be faked. He cares about you regardless
of who you are and what you are. He can do
what he has to do and he doesn't lose your
respect. LaVell is always LaVell. He is what he is.
There's no hidden agenda with him."

By the next fall, Kozlowski was back on campus. After a redshirt season he was back in uniform. By 1984 he was helping BYU win the
national championship and carrying his coach
off the field. He played through 1985, when his
eligibility ran out and the Chicago Bears drafted
him.

"I went to BYU as a punk, and I left there as
a father and a husband and a grown-up for the
first time in my life," says Kozlowski. "A lot of
people were instrumental in that transformation.
But I wouldn't have even come back if it hadn't
been for the relationship I formed with LaVell
Edwards the semester I wasn't even there. The
semester he allowed me to grow up."

CHAPTER SEVEN

Relationships

The sign had been there all along, although I hadn't noticed it before. NO COLOREDS ALLOWED it read, in block letters, set in the window of an ice cream shop in Fort Lee, Virginia.

We were on our way home from the movies, two twenty-three-year-old ROTC second lieutenants with our wives. In quartermaster class I'd gotten to know Steve, who sat next to me, and we found we had a lot in common. Same age, same rank, both recently married. After class one Friday he called his wife, I called mine, and the four of us went to the movies. On the walk home, I suggested we stop for some ice cream.

Steve and his wife didn't know what to say.

"We can't," they finally said.

"Why not?" I persisted with all the naiveté of one who had grown up in Orem, Utah.

Then I saw the sign.

It was the first time in my life I'd come face to face with racial prejudice. To me, the irony was overwhelming. The ROTC unit at Fort Lee was filled with black soldiers, many of them from the college next door. Virginia State, practically across the street from the base, was an all-black school with a big ROTC program. Steve was from Virginia State and he'd been born and raised in the area. I thought how odd it was—here I was a farm kid from Utah, two thousand miles away, and I could walk into that ice cream shop on Main Street like I owned the place. But Steve had grown up there—and he couldn't.

Even more odd to me was that Steve could go to Korea to fight for his country, which he would do in a matter of weeks, but he wasn't welcome inside certain places in his home country.

A decade or so later, when I watched television film clips of the civil rights marches and the protests and the riots in the South, I had a perspective that, unpleasant as it was, all that turmoil had to happen. The fight was for the freedom to be treated the same as anyone else, no better, no worse.

I feel strongly about that and always have: that people should be treated as individuals, not as a member of this race or that race, or, for that matter, a member of this religion or that religion, or of this team or that team.

Over the years we've had a lot of racial diversity on our football teams at BYU, as diverse, probably, as you'll find anywhere. We've had Tongans and Samoans directly from the islands, and we've had Polynesians born in America who have never been to the homeland of their ancestors. We've had native Americans, we've had blacks, and we've had whites from any number of ethnic backgrounds. We've had players from the inner cities to the mill towns, from Los Angeles to Beaver, Utah, from the East to the West and everything in between. We've had LDS kids and we've had non-LDS kids.

Just observing this "melting pot," watching it work, has been as rewarding as anything I've done in coaching. I've gotten a lot of satisfaction from knowing that the only time race has been any kind of an issue at BYU was when the dissension came from without, not from within.

Fortunately, racial discrimination against BYU has decreased over the years. I was an assistant coach when it was at its peak in the late 1960s. At the time, the LDS Church did not grant the priesthood to blacks, and feelings over that issue sometimes spilled over onto the football field. On a trip to San Jose State in 1968, the manager of our hotel woke up Tommy Hudspeth and myself. He said a bomb threat had been phoned in to the hotel switchboard—someone was angry about the Church's policy concerning the blacks and wanted to send a message. The police came, and we all sat in Tom's room at about one o'clock in the morning trying to decide what to do. After some investigation, the police concluded it was just a scare tactic and eventually decided not to wake up the team and evacuate. Apparently it was just a hoax because nothing happened, but the next night at the game I saw a football field surrounded by armed policemen for the first time.

Not long after that came the "Black 13" incident at Wyoming, where the black players on the Wyoming team refused to play against us because the coach wouldn't let them wear black arm bands. The remaining Wyoming players used that as a rallying cry and really hammered us that day, 40 to 7. But in the end the experience proved to be unsettling for the Wyoming football program, and they didn't win another game the rest of the season.

Other schools, such as Stanford, adopted policies that they wouldn't play BYU, policies that I found hypocritical since some of the schools involved had long histories of denying blacks, or African-Americans, admission to their schools. At one time in America's history of higher education, segregation was more of a rule than an exception. Such had never been the case at BYU. There was no restriction on admissions to blacks or to any other race. We were being discriminated against for a religious principle, for something we had absolutely no control over. To me that seemed as prejudiced as that sign in the ice cream shop in Virginia.

I was involved in recruiting the first black to come to BYU to play football, a twenty-six-year-old bus driver and member of the LDS Church in Chicago named Paul Devine. Tommy Hudspeth decided we should recruit Paul, and as the recruiting coordinator I was sent to Chicago to visit with Paul and his wife. When I got off the plane there were TV cameras waiting in the terminal. The media had been tipped off that BYU was recruiting a black athlete.

It wasn't that there'd ever been any kind of institutional edict that we couldn't recruit blacks. We just never had. There had been black students at BYU, and that had included a few black athletes, but mostly they had been on the track team and they were African-born blacks, not native-born Americans. By the '60s the mood had shifted sufficiently that the races were crossing borders. That's what the meeting between myself and Paul Devine was all about. Since he was a member of the Church, he seemed to be a good recruit to start crossing those borders. There weren't many blacks in Utah Valley, but there were a few Mormons.

Paul hadn't played since high school, so there was a question as to how fast he would—or could—get back into playing shape. But we had to make a start—in the world of major college athletics in the 1960s you weren't paying attention if you hadn't noticed that black athletes were a major part of the landscape, and they would only become more so.

Paul Devine and his wife enrolled at BYU the next year, although he never did play football in Provo. He transferred to Ricks College and did play there. He moved to California after he graduated. His relationship with BYU has always been excellent. A couple of years ago Paul's son was an outstanding high school prospect, and we were one of a number of Division I schools that recruited him. He chose to play elsewhere, but Paul was very supportive of BYU football.

COMPATIBILITY RECRUITING

Since Paul Devine we've had a continuous line of black players at BYU, yet there's never been an issue made about it—either way. I think a lot of the reason for that is we've never made an issue out of it ourselves. We haven't looked at it in racial terms. We've never operated on a quota system. We've never felt that there's a certain number of black players we should have—or brown or yellow or white players, for that matter. My feeling is that we try to find kids who can play and who can be compatible with the BYU environment. Period.

Over the years, that approach has taken a lot of guesswork out of our recruiting. It's really quite simple. If it appears that a player, no matter how talented and no matter where he comes from, just isn't going to be suited to the BYU environment, for whatever reasons, then it doesn't make sense, for either the player or for us, to pursue him. On the other hand, if it does appear he'll be suited to the environment, we'll go after him.

That's the issue: compatibility. It has never been black or white or LDS or non-LDS. It's lifestyle. People will try to make it a religious thing, or something racial, but that has nothing to do with it. It comes down to a lifestyle choice. A player coming to BYU needs to decide if he'll be comfortable with the lifestyle that is already in place. If he knows up front what's expected, if he understands he's expected to sign a code of conduct, if he knows he's expected to take religion classes, and he doesn't have a problem with any of the above, then he's made a decision that he's going to be compatible with the lifestyle here. We try to be completely up front about all of that because that's the issue that's most important.

There are times when you can sense that it's just not going to work very well, when you know there's going to be conflict. Early on, I used to kid myself that a player's attitude might change, but over time I've become more of a realist. On occasion I have told recruits, after visiting with them, that I think they might have a difficult time at BYU and wished them well in seeking another university. That's not easy—telling a talented young football player, one who obviously has a great future ahead of him in the game—that he'd probably be better off elsewhere. But adjustments to college can be hard enough—just getting to class, just growing-up things—without having to change your attitudes about lifestyle.

For that and any number of other reasons, recruiting is more difficult at BYU; there's no question about that.

But recruiting has never been a problem for me. It's never been something I dread. A lot of that has to do with the fact that it's a people business, and meeting people in a recruiting situation—essentially offering a free college education—is not at all unpleasant. Ninety-nine percent of the time I'll make a home visit to those recruits we've committed to sign (they might not be committed, but we are). I've never felt I'm particularly great in a home. They'll never tell stories about me like they do about Woody Hayes or some of the other legendary recruiters. But for the most part I enjoy the visits. I enjoy meeting people. Mainly I try to sit down and listen. I've found that people like to talk. Sometimes I've heard reports that this family or that family really enjoyed their visit with me. And I'll think to myself, "But I didn't even say anything."

Selling the parents is what works. It would be great for us if the

NCAA allowed parents to visit the campus. The parents can visit, but it has to be at their own expense. Sometimes a recruit will bring his parents; often that will clinch the deal. That's how we got Jamal Willis. We flew him in from Las Vegas, and his parents drove up to join him. The parents aren't LDS, but they're very religious and they thought the BYU atmosphere would be good for their son. It's amazing how much more persuasive parents can be than a football coach.

Once a player is here, the opportunity to develop a significant relationship begins. I've always felt the key to that is making sure that you treat each individual as a person who happens to be a football player instead of the other way around. To be effective, relationships need to be on an individual basis. Because of that, as head coach I choose to deal with the players, for the most part, on a one-on-one level. I don't get up and talk to the team a whole lot, but I do spend a lot of time talking to the team members individually. A lot of our discussions aren't even about football, but we're talking about other things that are important to them.

Establishing a relationship takes time. I'm sure if you asked a lot of our players when they're freshmen, they wouldn't have a lot to say about their head coach, other than that he doesn't say much and they wonder what he does. But before they're through it's practically guaranteed that we'll have a number of experiences that bring us together. When the situation arises that they need to talk to me, I want to be there. I never close the door to my office—other than for a private conversation—and I never will. I want my office to always be accessible; I want to always be accessible. That's why I keep a jar filled with lemon drops inside my office. I haven't eaten half a dozen lemon drops the whole time I've been at BYU. I don't even like lemon drops. But I have players who won't pass the door without coming in and grabbing one or two.

EQUAL TREATMENT MEANS DIFFERENT TREATMENT

I want that kind of open, casual atmosphere because it helps me to get to know the players. Getting to know them as individuals is essential to knowing how best to treat them as individuals. No two are going to have the same needs. It just isn't going to work if you treat them all the same. If you're going to treat people fairly and equally, you have to treat them differently.

Even with your own children you realize that. You need to treat them differently in their own areas. You can't motivate them in exactly the same way; you can't discipline them exactly the same way. Children need to be raised as individuals, not as a group. It's the same for football players. They need to be treated—and coached—as individuals, not as a group.

Just as I've never wanted to have coaches on the staff that are all clones of each other, I haven't wanted to have a team of players who are all alike. Variety is key to a well-rounded football team, and if you're going to have variety then you're going to have to be prepared to deal with different personalities. I've never wanted to stifle anyone's individuality, and I've tried to create an atmosphere that promotes that.

I think that's why we've had very few serious problems, despite the fact there are a lot of rules and requirements at BYU. As long as it's within the rules, individuality isn't discouraged, it's encouraged. Jim McMahon is a good example of that. Jim had his own agenda, but to tell the truth—and contrary, I'm sure, to what a lot of people might think—he was one of the easier ones to coach and get along with. He was a great student of football, he loved to compete, his teammates really liked him, and he had almost no ego. We didn't try to turn him into somebody other than who he was—and he didn't try to change anyone else. He wasn't at all difficult to deal with.

To be consistent with this "to treat them equally, treat them differently" philosophy, it's important to never lose sight of an individual's personal dignity. This can be especially important in the area of discipline—a point that was driven home particularly hard to me the day Junior Filiaga slugged the referee.

Junior Filiaga was a defensive lineman for us whose emotions got the best of him in a 1980 game at Utah State. Frustrated by what he felt was excessive holding by the Aggie offensive line, and by a Utah State four-touchdown rally that made it necessary for our starters to reenter the game in the fourth quarter, he momentarily lost control and attacked the official—something that in all my years of football I had not seen happen.

But it happened then and, needless to say, it left me stunned. I wasn't sure what to do. There was no manual for this one. They'd never covered this in summer coaching clinics.

When I saw it happen I just kind of froze. I got a sick feeling in my stomach. I knew this was serious. I knew there were going to be severe repercussions. Luckily, the blow had been more glancing than direct, and the official was basically shaken up but okay. No bones were broken. That brought a sigh of relief. But my concern quickly shifted to what would happen to the player. Would he be banned for life?

There was all kinds of commotion when the game ended. I went on the radio and the first thing Paul James, our play-by-play announcer, asked for was a comment on "the incident." Then the phone lines opened up for the postgame call-in show, and that's all anyone wanted to talk about.

That was the last thing I wanted to do—talk. And I said so. I told Paul there was nothing more to say or analyze, and other than acknowledging what had happened, I wouldn't make any more reference to what had happened, at least not at that point. A mistake had been made and it had to be dealt with. I left it at that.

I didn't want to throw gas on a fire. I knew who I was dealing with. I knew Junior tended to be extremely sensitive and emotional. He had an ability to be loving, kissing, fighting, and making up, all within ten minutes. Just by looking at him, I knew Junior was completely remorseful before the game even ended. I knew he was as embarrassed as he could possibly be. If there was any way for him to undo what he'd done he'd do it, but of course he couldn't.

I never did chew him out. I didn't have to. He'd taken care of that himself before I ever got to him in the locker room. What was left for me was to try to understand what had happened, what may have contributed to the punch. I realized that as much as anything it had been a reflex action. In the culture Junior had been raised in, physical responses like that, right or wrong, were a way of life. This wasn't to exonerate what he had done, but to illuminate it and put it in a context that made it more understandable. It made it possible for me to deal with him on that basis, which really was the only fair way to deal with him. When we talked, that's what we talked about—about why he did what he did. He didn't get defensive and try to say he was justified for what he'd done, and I didn't get offensive and try to make a public spectacle out of him by vilifying him.

Junior was suspended for the rest of the season by the league office, which I felt was the appropriate action. Under certain circumstances I'm sure that could have been the end of him as a football player. But there were enough positive relationships between Junior Filiaga and BYU football that he came back the next season, as a senior, and played for us the whole year without further incident.

People should not only be allowed to make their mistakes, they should also be allowed to make their amends. More often than not, if they're allowed to they'll make those amends on their own. They don't need someone to lower the boom on them. They'll lower it on themselves. They don't always need a head coach to spell out their errors.

There was an incident a couple of years ago in Hawaii when our tight end, Byron Rex, happened to be on TV when he shouted insults at the Hawaii fans. As with the Junior Filiaga incident, there was considerable public and media attention. A few days later, I made the comment that whatever we did in the way of discipline, it wouldn't amount to much when compared to what Byron's mother had already done to him. It was a facetious comment in a way, meant to defuse a potentially volatile situation I didn't want to see blown out of proportion. But in another way it wasn't facetious at all. No matter what we did, discipline-wise, it wasn't going to have the impact of whatever his mother said.

If I hadn't known about the close relationships Byron had with his parents, I wouldn't have been able to confidently make that statement. But I did know of his close relationship with his parents, and I had good reason to suspect that his discipline had pretty much been taken care of. We suspended him for a game, to send a message to the team that that kind of behavior wasn't tolerable. But as far as Byron Rex was concerned, I believe that message had already been delivered.

Just as it's true that all players are not created equally, it's also true that all players cannot be motivated in the same way. It is in the area of motivation that I think you can be most helpful as a coach, but only if you've done your homework. Sooner or later, if you've paid attention, you'll be in a position to help. If your players know that you've taken the time to get to know them and understand them—and that you'll work with them—then you'll not only have created an atmosphere conducive to strong and lasting relationships, but you'll also have created an atmosphere conducive to good team chemistry. For a football team to be successful, it's essential that the players be willing to work together no matter what their differences, no matter where they've come from or who they are. Chemistry starts at the top. If there's a feeling of fairness in the coaches' office, it's going to get transferred to the playing field.

Some of my most satisfying experiences as a coach—and I'm sure this must be true for most coaches—have been watching the camaraderie that develops on the different teams as they come together.

Another satisfying part of the job is being able to maintain relationships over the years. Relationships don't dissolve once a player's eligibility runs out. I not only correspond or visit regularly with those people who coached me, but I'm also able to correspond and visit regularly with those people I've coached.

That's always been important to me—to keep in touch. Sometimes I won't see or hear from a player or a coach for years, but then there will be a note or a call and we'll catch up with each other again. It's one of the great benefits of being in this business. You have this huge extended family, and it keeps getting bigger. It's especially satisfying when you find out—and sometimes it's not until years later—that you've had a positive impact on someone's life. I know that countless numbers of people have had a positive impact on mine.

Keeping in touch really came home to me at the ten-year reunion for our national championship team. I hadn't seen most of the players since we'd won the championship, and I was surprised at how emotional I got when I saw them again and felt the spirit they had together. It was a marvelous weekend that rekindled some very strong and special friendships.

Most days I'll devote at least some time to keeping in touch. It doesn't take all that much time, really, just a little effort. But you do have to give it a certain priority. I don't spend a lot of time in the film room, for one thing, which frees me up. A lot of coaches will watch film almost around the clock. That's fine, of course, and sometimes I feel I'd be better off if I did too. But I don't particularly like doing it. I've always liked working with people more than I've liked working with film.

Luckily for me, I picked a business that places a high priority on working with others and developing lasting friendships. That's something you can definitely take with you.

First Things First

Vince Dooley, the head football coach at the University of Georgia, had a time-management problem. With the time he had, he knew it was going to be hard to manage.

He'd signed a national network TV contract that moved Georgia's game with Clemson from the second Saturday in September to Labor Day night. The game between the two previous national champions—Georgia in 1980, Clemson in 1981—portended record ratings and serious national exposure. Prime time on a holiday. There was no telling how many potential recruits might be watching. It was a deal Dooley and the Bulldogs couldn't turn down.

Changing the schedule had turned the following game at home against Brigham Young into a problem, however. Georgia would have to play in South Carolina late Monday night, travel back home to Athens on Tuesday, and then have just three days to prepare for Saturday's game with a well-rested BYU.

Then Dooley got a brainstorm. As he looked at BYU's schedule, he noticed that the Cougars had an open week the next weekend—the weekend Georgia had originally scheduled Clemson.

If he could talk BYU into moving the game back a week, he could see a potential win-win situation—for Georgia. And he had a hole card he was prepared to play. He and the Cougars' head coach, LaVell Edwards, were the best of friends. They'd known each other for years. They traveled together in the off season, they played golf together, their wives shopped together. He and Barbara had been to Provo and stayed with LaVell and Patti.

"I decided it was time to put our friendship to the test," says Dooley. "And LaVell failed miserably."

The BYU coach's reply to his friend was two words long: "No way."

"I gave him the whole story, how I'd noticed his schedule was such that he didn't have a game the following week and neither did we," says Dooley. "So I asked him: Would he go ahead and play the following week and not put us at such a disadvantage? I added that if they would be willing to make that change, I was sure we could offer an incentive to their athletic department.

"LaVell told me he wasn't interested in any incentives for the athletic department. He said he wanted to play as scheduled. He said he was most anxious to put us at a disadvantage.

"Of course I'd have done the same thing," says Dooley. "Good friends or not, there's a limit and this was beyond it. LaVell didn't let his friendship with me overrule doing his job. He wanted to win. He had that ability to keep it separate. To not make the game personal. If you're going to take things personally, then you're not going to have LaVell Edwards' record. He's going to do everything he can to beat you. Then, afterward, he'll go to dinner with you."

"You know, there are coaches who would have changed that game," says Dooley. "They would have thought of themselves first and their program second. But LaVell doesn't let things get to him that shouldn't. He didn't have any problem with me asking him to switch that game, and he didn't have any problem telling me no. He knew it wouldn't destroy our friendship, and if it did, it wasn't much of a friendship anyway. I think the great understanding he has of human nature has a lot to do with why he's been successful for so long.

"It's like the year BYU won the national championship by beating Michigan in the bowl game. Michigan had a very average football team that year, and there was some criticism about that. Barry Switzer at Oklahoma said that of course BYU deserved to win the national championship because they'd done something only five other teams had been able to do that season—beat Michigan.

"A lot of people might take exception to something like that; they might take it personally. But you know, LaVell enjoyed that line more than anyone. When he heard what Barry had said he had a big laugh. And the funniest part was, he had a national championship to go along with it."

CHAPTER EIGHT

Expectations

In the family I grew up in, there was no family "mission statement" on how we were supposed to act. There were no lists on the walls of what we expected to accomplish. But *within* the walls was a different story. Within the walls there were all kinds of expectations—expectations that you understood even though they weren't always verbalized or openly discussed. If you were an "Edwards" there were certain things that were expected of you. It was a big family, and since I was in the middle these expectations were well established by the time I came along.

I was fortunate that my family had healthy expectations and provided strong support. That made it easy for me. All I had to do was choose to follow the path that had already been set.

It's expectations that, in large measure, drive families, companies, football teams, political parties, social clubs, even churches. Virtually any pursuit, from trying to win an Olympic medal to trying to land on the moon, is tied to a certain set of expectations. The "right" set of expectations—those that are realistic and reachable—drive success and satisfaction; while the "wrong" set of expectations—those that are unreachable and unrealistic—only drive disappointment and failure.

In many ways, BYU football functions much like the family I grew up in. There are few specific goals. Other than our yearly goal of winning the league title—which I believe is a tangible goal that allows us to focus on something we have total control over—ours has never been a football program that's focused on precise goals. And yet, we've been able to reach what anyone would label as worthy goals, and that ties back into our expectation level.

That's what's behind BYU football being able to reach heights that at one time would have been outlandish to even think about. It's all been due to steadily increasing expectations. As we kept expecting to get better, over time we found ourselves arriving at places we'd never been before.

Such as the national championship.

EXPECTING TO WIN

On paper, we had no business winning the national championship in 1984. For one thing, there were plenty of other very good major college football teams that year, and all of them had to lose somehow, someway, to somebody, to give us a shot even if we somehow managed to win all of our games.

For another thing, we weren't as talented as we'd been the year before—or, for that matter, as we'd be the year after. Our 1983 team had set a standard as the most prolific offensive team in NCAA history by averaging 584.2 yards per game. Steve Young was the quarterback, and the only game we lost all season was the opener at Baylor, by four points. We won eleven straight games after that, including the Holiday Bowl.

A year after the national championship, our 1985 team would have maybe the best defense we've ever had. That's the year Jason Buck, who would go on to win the Outland Trophy a year later, transferred from Ricks College and joined Shawn Knight on the defensive line.

In 1984 we were in something of a transition. Particularly at quarterback. Steve Young was gone and Robbie Bosco, who had played very little in two years as his backup, had replaced him. There were other glaring holes to fill, such as at tight end, since we lost Gordon Hudson after an All-American career. Reflecting those holes, none of the preseason polls mentioned BYU.

So if you just looked at the personnel picture and the stat sheets, you wouldn't choose 1984 as the year we'd win the national championship. But we did win it that year, and I think it had to do with two significant intangibles. One was luck—and there's no question we had a lot of it that year. The other was our own expectations.

Nobody on that team thought we *couldn't* win it.

As the season progressed, so did our expectations. You could practically feel it. Without the expectations, I'm convinced we'd never have made it. With them, we put ourselves in a position to win it all.

Like I said, luck had a lot to do with it too. If every challenger that year hadn't lost when it was supposed to, almost as if it were on cue, the national championship would never have found its way to Provo. The spot at the top of the polls would have never been available to us. We could have won all our games and still finished second or third or fourth. And if we hadn't been able to go through an entire year with only two significant injuries—one to receiver Adam Haysbert (and he missed only one game) and the other to lineman Craig Garrick—we might not have been so fortunate, either.

But all the challengers did lose, one by one, and we did manage to go through an entire season practically injury-free—and as we did, the expectations within our team only continued to grow.

The start helped.

If the oddsmakers had been right, we would have been out of the race by the time the first weekend was history. Our opener was at Pittsburgh, against a University of Pittsburgh team ranked Number 3 in the preseason polls. If that wasn't intimidating enough, ESPN, the cable TV sports network, picked that game to make its live broadcasting debut. BYU at Pittsburgh made history as ESPN's first-ever live football broadcast.

We certainly didn't go into that game thinking that this would be the start of an undefeated season that would lead to a national championship. But as the game wore on, and the prospect of winning began to look at least possible, a dim kind of realization began to surface. If we could beat third-ranked Pittsburgh at Pittsburgh, and do it on national TV, just how much harder could it get?

It also helped that we had to come back to earn that win. We never got in a position where we could get nervous about protecting any kind of a comfortable lead. This was one of those games that was close enough that we were able to concentrate on just playing football. Robbie, in particular, settled down after one of the shakiest debuts in BYU quarterbacking history. Not that it was unexpected. Before the game I'd approached Robbie in the locker room—I knew he'd had a hard time sleeping and was having trouble keeping food down.

"How you doing?" I asked.

"I'm all right," he answered, but his answer was belied by his voice, which was barely above a whisper. He sounded like a boxer who'd already gone the distance with three broken ribs.

Our new starting quarterback opened the season by throwing a pass that was still gaining altitude as it passed over our heads on the sidelines. When we first saw the pass coming toward us we started to duck. Then we realized we didn't need to. The ball landed about four rows up in the stands.

His next pass would have probably been intercepted if it hadn't hit his own lineman in the back of the helmet. After that we punted and Steve Young's heir apparent came over to the sidelines.

"Just keep throwing," I told Robbie. I think just knowing that he wasn't going to be the first BYU starter whose career lasted one series helped settle him down.

We generated only enough offense for a field goal in the opening half, but that was enough for a 3–0 lead because our defense kept Pittsburgh out of the end zone, an effort climaxed with a goal-line stand that left Pitt on the one-foot line as the half ended. Buoyed by that defensive stand, you could sense the mood shift in the locker room. Our players had an attitude that they could win here, in Pittsburgh, on ESPN.

It would get worse, however, before it got better again. Robbie threw a couple of interceptions early in the second half—one of them after the ball bounced off Glen Kozlowski's shoulder pads—and both resulted in Pittsburgh touchdowns. They had us 14–3. That's when we could have packed it in. That's when a lot of teams would have packed it in.

But not this team. This wasn't a team that flinched when things got tough. I'd had an indication of that six months earlier during spring practice. We had a scrimmage in the stadium one Saturday, and about a third of the way into it a storm blew in. It was one of those northers that come out of nowhere. Just like that, the temperature dropped, it started to rain hard—and an interesting thing happened. All of a sudden the players started playing harder. We had our best practice of the spring. I drove home that night and told Patti I couldn't put my finger on it and it didn't make sense to get too hopeful because of all the players we'd lost, but I had a feeling about this team.

We managed to score twice (another field goal and a touchdown) but still only pulled within two points, 14–12, when our try for a two-point conversion failed after the touchdown. The score stayed that way for a while. We'd hold them and then they'd hold us. Not that I was happy for them, since I would have preferred a four-touchdown lead, but ESPN had to be pleased. Their debut game was going to the wire.

When we got the ball with just a couple of minutes left, our hope was to move far enough down the field to try another field goal. Our kicker that year was Lee Johnson and he had great range, so we were hoping to get past midfield and give him a chance. With that in mind, and only a little over a minute left, we called a 62 on a third and four. A 62 is a passing play that calls for the receivers to cross. It typically attracts man-to-man coverage with the free safety, as usual, there to help defend farther down the field. What the quarterback wants to see is the safety committing to one of the wide receivers as they cross at midfield; then the quarterback will pass the other way. In a best-case scenario, the receiver left with man-to-man coverage gets a step on his defender and breaks downfield on a post route, beyond the defense.

That's exactly what happened, and Robbie, his nerves by now settled, picked it up. He wasn't a rattled quarterback anymore. Now he was competing. As he would time and again that season, he turned everything over to his instincts.

When he saw that safety move up, he just looked upfield and let the ball go. Adam Haysbert had a step on the cornerback covering him. He caught the ball in stride and went in for the touchdown. We went for two, made it, and now had a 20–14 lead. When our defense held in the final minute, we'd escaped our visit to the Top 10 and national television with a win.

One thing simply led to another that season. We came home and beat Baylor, 47–13. That's when the Baylor coach, Grant Teaff, said, "I don't know if we're that bad or they're that good." Before the game, in a players-only meeting, the team had talked openly about the possibility of winning the national championship. Their strategy was to win them all and then see what might happen.

Five games really stand out in my mind when I think of that 1984 season. One, of course, was the Pittsburgh game, one was at Hawaii in our conference opener four games into the season, one was against Wyoming at homecoming, one was at Utah, and the fifth was the Holiday Bowl game against Michigan. In each of these games, the positive expectations of the team especially stood out.

At Hawaii, we won 18–13 in a game we could easily have lost if it hadn't been for a play by our safety, Kyle Morrell. Hawaii had a third down next to the goal line. They had only a couple of inches to go for the touchdown. They ran a quarterback sneak, the kind of play that will work probably ninety-nine times out of a hundred in that kind of a situation. But just as the ball was snapped, Kyle was on top of the quarterback, grabbing him by the jersey and pulling him backward, away from the goal line.

It's amazing what players will think of on their own. As he explained afterward, Kyle guessed that they'd run the quarterback sneak, and his plan was to try to jump over the Hawaii center the second he hiked the ball. His timing had to be perfect for it to work. But he reasoned that if it wasn't, all they could do was call him offsides and assess the penalty, which meant moving the ball half the distance to the goal line. Since the ball was already practically resting on the line, what was the risk? Maybe an inch?

But his timing was perfect and now, on fourth down, Hawaii had about a yard to go. They kicked a field goal instead of going for the touchdown, which put them up, but only by two. We came right back and scored. We really dodged a bullet that night.

Wyoming was having kind of an off year, but when they came to Provo to play in our homecoming game, it seemed as if they scored every time they had the ball. They'd obviously done a great job of scouting. Every time we went into a certain defense they'd counter it perfectly. Luckily, we were also scoring, but it came down to the last minute and we had to protect a 41–38 lead. That was one of those hard days you have to survive if you're going to be successful, when everything goes wrong and you still manage to hang on.

In the second to the last game of the regular season we played at Utah and won, 24–14. It was a very tough game, tougher than the score would make you think. We were ranked third in the nation at the time, behind Nebraska and South Carolina, and there was a lot of pressure that went with that ranking—along with the usual pressure of playing the Utes in Salt Lake City. While we were winning, South Carolina was getting beaten by Navy, a team that wasn't ranked, and Nebraska was getting beaten at Oklahoma.

In 1984 the new rankings didn't come out each week until Monday afternoon. After Monday's practice I was sitting with some of the coaches in a car in the Smith Fieldhouse parking lot, listening to the sports on KSL radio. That's how we got the news that BYU was ranked Number 1.

We beat Utah State in our final regular season game and carried—some might say "dragged"—that Number 1 ranking into our bowl game against Michigan in San Diego. We were definitely the team to beat in the national championship picture, but we still had to get past Michigan and then hope we could remain Number 1 in the final polls, which were to be conducted after all the bowls were played.

For a while, it didn't look like we were going to keep up our end of the bargain. For one thing, the season without injuries was over. Robbie's knee was badly damaged after a late hit just nine minutes into the Michigan game, and he had to go to the training room for treatment. For another thing, we decided to play as if every down was for, well, for the national championship. The pressure that hadn't gotten to us before seemed to be getting to us now.

But then Robbie came back out of the training room and limped onto the field. Nothing was going to keep him out of this game. His courage was contagious, and his comeback got us our first touchdown, giving us a 7–0 lead.

But something else was contagious. Turnovers. By the end of the third quarter we had five of them—two interceptions and three fumbles. Not surprisingly, we weren't ahead. We trailed 17–10 with a gimpy quarterback and twelve minutes left to play.

But the team that liked it when things got tough came through one last time. That fourth quarter was as satisfying as anything I've been involved with in football. Robbie led us on two scoring drives, one for seventy yards and the other for eighty, and our defense held Michigan to *minus* three yards in offense. And we didn't have a turnover. The winning play, it turned out, was a halfback pass from Robbie to Kelly Smith with just over a minute remaining.

Later on it hit me just how appropriate that play was as it applied to the BYU football program. The play itself, the H-option, was a basic play in our passing offense. It called for the halfback to run into the flat and look for the ball. If he saw that the quarterback was being rushed, he was to turn and go deep, beyond the coverage. Kelly did just that, and Robbie, in the face of a heavy rush, got him the ball. Touchdown. They ran that play like it was something they'd done at least a thousand times in practice—which they had.

Year in, year out, plays like that have been the lifeblood of the BYU passing game, just as players like Kelly Smith and Robbie Bosco have been the lifeblood of the program. Kelly was originally a walk-on from Beaver, Utah, who hung in the program, paid his dues, and finally got playing time as a junior in 1984. As for Robbie, he was certainly typical of the kind of player we'd had at quarterback over the years—a hard worker who hadn't been highly recruited and who had patiently worked his way up through the system.

Those players, and that H-option play, were as representative of BYU football as you could get.

Because we beat Michigan by just a touchdown, 24–17, and because the strength of our schedule had become such an issue, a debate ensued about whether we would, or should, be Number 1 after the New Year's Day bowls were played. Bryant Gumbel said on the *Today* show that BYU played "Bo Diddley Tech," managing to upset both BYU and Bo Diddley, the blues musician, in one shot.

The controversy that began the day we moved to the top of the polls wound up generating more interest in BYU football than anything else in our history. As the season developed, writers and broadcasters from around the country came to Provo to see what we were all about. The exposure was tremendous. A lot of people learned a lot about BYU in just a few weeks' time. That adage about any publicity being good publicity as long as they spell your name right held true in this case. Virtually all of the publicity was good—and as far as I know, no one misspelled "BYU."

There was still a chance that second-ranked Oklahoma, the team that helped us get to Number 1 by beating Nebraska at the end of the regular season, could jump over us and move to Number 1 if it defeated Washington in the Orange Bowl. But in a season where everything fell into place for BYU, that wasn't going to happen. Washington won.

I was coaching the East-West Shrine Game in San Francisco when I got the word that the final polls had voted us Number 1. I'd asked the sports information director to let me know when anything was announced. He walked toward the field and held up his index finger. That's how I knew: BYU was the 1984 national champion.

We'd gone somewhere I'd never envisioned we would go.

PERPETUATING EXPECTATIONS

But we'd also gone somewhere that, deep down, I wasn't surprised about when we arrived. It wasn't that we knew we *would* be national champions at BYU as much as we knew we *could*. Our expectations hadn't held us back because our expectations were that we *could* beat the best, we *could* win if we found ourselves in that position. If the stars and the moon and the planets lined up a certain way, we could—and when they did, we did.

I've never done a study of how prevalent that kind of feeling is in programs across the country, but I'm sure if I did I'd find it in those programs that have sustained success. Once positive expectations get established, they become the undertow that pulls you along.

That feeling that says we won't be satisfied unless we succeed—and we expect to succeed—is of incalculable value. Failing to succeed won't change the world, but it won't leave us satisfied either. We expect more than that.

The beauty of positive expectations is that they tend to perpetuate themselves. In any football program, each year's team, as it searches for its own identity, is going to build on what the teams preceding it have done. If there's a tradition of never quite making it, then it's going to be easy to expect more of the same—and if there's a tradition of success, then it's going to be easy to expect more success.

The more success, the stronger the expectations and the more stable your program. You keep *expecting* to do well, and you keep on rolling. You have your ups and you have your downs, but your expectations don't ride that same roller coaster. Your expectations put you in a position where you can consistently be successful, where you'll allow yourself to win.

After we defeated Notre Dame in 1994 someone made a study of all our games since 1972. They found that, with the exception of Ohio State, every opponent we'd played at least three times we'd been able to beat at least once. Notre Dame was the latest example. We'd played the Irish in 1992 and 1993 and they defeated us both times, by similarly lopsided scores (42–16 and 45–20). Conventional wisdom would have suggested that the third time would be more of the same, particularly since they were nationally ranked, they were coming off a loss at Boston College, and the game was at Notre Dame.

If we'd based our expectations on our previous two games with Notre Dame we'd have been in trouble. But we hadn't treated either defeat as an end-of-the-world type thing. We'd actually gone on to win our league both years. With expectations more stable than any single win or loss, we were able to treat our third meeting with Notre Dame on an individual basis.

We lost twice to Penn State before finally winning, and we lost to Miami in the Orange Bowl before beating them early in the 1990 season in Provo, 28–21, when Miami was the defending national champion and ranked Number 1 in the nation. We were big underdogs in that game, but there was a tremendous amount of resolve with that team. The players spent the summer preparing themselves for the opportunity to bump off Number 1.

Preparation, of course, is the glue that ties expectations to results. The key to success is not to have the will to win as much as it is to have the will to prepare. It's easy to want to win. It's particularly easy to want to win on Saturday, when it's game day, when the stands are full of people, when the bands are playing, when the TV cameras are turned on. Who wouldn't want to win under those circumstances? Who can't get fired up and ready to go then?

But what about on Monday or Tuesday? Or what about in March? What about in the weight room on a hot morning in July?

People who are successful, and who sustain that success, prepare themselves for the opportunity to succeed—and then they aren't surprised when it happens. They expect it. Whether you call that goal setting or something else, I know it's been the real key to any good results we have realized. It's been our basic formula for success: Preparation and Expectations.

More than the national championship of 1984, more than any of the accomplishments by individual athletes or specific teams, it's been our ability to maintain our success, and our expectations, that's pleased me the most over the years. What we've learned through experience we've been able to consistently apply. I believe that once you create an environment where you expect to succeed, more often than not you will.

Triumph and Disaster

Paul Roach,
*former University of Wyoming coach,
now athletic director there*

They crossed the football field at Cougar Stadium under completely different circumstances. One had just won by two points; the other had just lost by four points. In college football those are the polar opposites. But they were similarly disarmed by the opposing coach. Ask Paul Roach or Rich Brooks for their impressions of LaVell Edwards and they'll both take you back to the first time they met him at midfield in Provo.

You can tell a lot about a coach by the way he shakes your hand—after a game.

Rich Brooks,
*former University of Oregon coach,
now with the NFL Rams*

• • •

Roach was midway into his first season as the head coach at the University of Wyoming in 1987. It was his first visit to Cougar Stadium and the sixty-six thousand fans who unfailingly fill the seats. Wyoming hadn't beaten the Cougars in Provo in eleven years, and he could see why. It was an intimidating place. He didn't expect to win this time, either, especially after BYU took a 14–0 lead in the first half.

But after that it was all Wyoming. The Cowboys scored twenty-nine points in the second half. BYU managed thirteen more of its own, but not until late in the fourth quarter, and when a two-point conversion try failed in the closing minutes, it added up to Wyoming 29, BYU 27. The sixty-six thousand were not happy.

Roach didn't think the BYU coach was going to be in much of a mood for pleasantries, either, as he walked onto the field for the traditional post-game handshake. A two-point loss. To a league member. At home. Foul moods have been summoned up by a lot less.

"LaVell never smiles on the sidelines anyway," says Roach. "I thought he might be a ferocious man by nature. I didn't know what to expect after this kind of a loss.

"But he stood there and shook my hand and said congratulations. He didn't talk very much about his team, and he praised our team. He said we'd put them to sleep and they didn't wake up until the fourth quarter. And by then it was too late.

"What I came to find out was that he was the same guy, win or lose," says Roach, who developed a close friendship with Edwards after that initial meeting. "He isn't critical. He isn't a whiner. He accepts what happens. I think that's why he's always been just one of the guys in the WAC, despite the fact that he's won so much. He's never, ever, tried to lord it over anybody, and when he loses, he accepts it.

"A unique thing I discovered about LaVell Edwards," Roach continues, "is that he's one of the few coaches in all my coaching experience, both as an assistant and as a head coach, whom you could have a good conversation with *before* the game. We'd talk about the weather, or about what happened the year before, or the personalities of our quarterbacks, or our families, or the importance of the game we were about to play. It didn't matter what it was; it was always a genuine visit that wasn't filled with the normal clichés that coaches will say before a game.

"I have to say, after watching him on the sidelines from afar for many years, he turned out to be a completely different guy from what I thought."

• • •

Rich Brooks saw sure victory give way to sudden defeat, and he was not at all happy about it. Losing a nineteen-point lead in the fourth quarter was one thing, but losing it to what he called "mysterious flags" only made it that much harder to take.

"Worst officiating I'd ever seen," says Brooks, the head coach at the University of Oregon. "We're in complete control, and then they throw those flags and we lose in the last thirty seconds, 45–41. I was extremely upset, to say the least."

Upset enough that by the time he got to midfield and met his close friend LaVell Edwards, the coach of the BYU team that, along with the referees, had just beaten him, he was just warming up.

"I know he'd never seen me like that before," says Brooks. "We'd done a lot of things together over the years. We'd coached together in Japan and in some other All-Star games, and we'd played a lot of golf. But I know he'd never seen me really angry. And I *was* angry. I told him how upset I was over the officiating. I told him I thought we'd been robbed. I know I stunned him with my outburst."

A lot of friendships might have ended right there, or at least been put on hold for a while.

"But all LaVell did was pause for a minute after I'd had my say," Brooks recalls. "And then he said, 'Oh, c'mon, Rich, I don't know what you're so upset about. You see these guys once a year. I get them every week.'"

Even the coach who had just been left in a heap at the side of the road by the evil officiating had to laugh.

"He's the most even-tempered, unflappable guy I've ever been around in the coaching profession," says Brooks. "I know I'm not like that. I don't know many who are.

"He puts things in perspective better than a lot of us do. He doesn't respond with outbursts or anger. He just stays on an even keel. We play golf together, and he's an excellent golfer. Most of the time he scores really well. But occasionally he shoots in the nineties and, honestly, you couldn't tell. You couldn't tell if he's shooting a ninety or a seventy-six. He doesn't let either one ruin his day."

"A lot of coaches would like to be like he is," says Brooks. "Whatever happens, he handles it. He takes it in stride. What you see is what you get. I don't know that LaVell Edwards has an enemy. When you act like he does, it's hard to have any."

BYU and the University of Utah have been going at it for almost a century now. It doesn't matter what it is—debate, ballroom dancing, basketball, football, fusion experiments. You name it, the competition is extreme. It may very well be the most intense college rivalry in America. Think about it, do Michigan and Ohio State or Nebraska and Oklahoma—to name two of the great college football rivalries—go at it as hard in basketball as they do in football? Do they go at it like BYU and Utah do in everything?

CHAPTER NINE

Nothing Personal

It's a rivalry that is fierce, fervent, intense, passionate, and powerful—and that list leaves out the adjectives that can incite riots. To paraphrase former Utah coach Wayne Howard (in complete context, I believe, which is to say without rancor), BYU and Utah don't like each other very much.

But I don't have any problem understanding why Utah fans, in general, haven't taken that out on LaVell Edwards. Over the years I've tried never to say or do anything that's going to make them want to hold anything against me personally.

I've never had an agenda to win a popularity contest with opposing fans, at Utah or anywhere else. I don't *try* to be liked. I don't spend my days doing things to gain their favor. I've never had an agent and never will have. I'd be a terrible promoter.

I love playing Utah. I love the whole rivalry. I love the kind of intense competition it fosters. I've never forgotten what Eddie Kimball, who coached BYU football in the '30s and '40s and then was athletic director for a number of years, told me not long after I'd taken over as head coach. We'd beaten Utah in two or three straight games, and I was telling Eddie that it was nice to have done that, but I thought the Utes were going through a slump and those teams we'd beaten hadn't really been very good. Eddie, who hadn't ever beaten Utah (he was serving in World War II in 1942, the first season BYU ever defeated the Utes), looked at me and said, "Now listen to me, LaVell. Don't ever lose sight of how important it is to beat Utah!" Then, in case I hadn't heard him, he said it again.

(I would have a similar experience in Austin, Texas, following a win we had over the University of Texas at their home field. Bill Yeoman, the former University of Houston coach and a good friend, was in the stands. As we were talking after the game I said something like, "Well, that's not a normal Texas team we beat" and Bill, who had played Texas dozens of times, said, "Hey, don't ever lose sight of the fact that you beat Texas in Austin. Do you know how often that's happened in the last fifty years?" I saw his point, too.)

But while I've tried to never forget what Eddie Kimball told me about the importance of beating Utah (and so far I haven't), I've also tried to never turn BYU-Utah into something that it's not—and that's into something personal.

It isn't that way only with Utah. It's an overall attitude I have. I try to never get personal about things that aren't personal in the first place. I know I couldn't survive for very long if I did, let alone enjoy what I'm doing. I don't think anybody can. I choose to respect who I'm playing and take care of my own team's business, and that's where it stops. I am not in the habit, and hopefully never will be, of doing or saying anything designed *not* to respect and get along with others, especially our opponents.

If I can be successful at that, then I'm freed up to enjoy a great rivalry like BYU-Utah. It becomes a positive thing for me and for the program I'm involved with. It does not become something that's negative, detracting, and unpleasant.

And it's also going to allow me to be the best football coach I can be. There is no room in effective coaching for grudges, vendettas, revenge—or for gloating, for that matter.

PLAYING WITH A VENGEANCE

People often ask if we're going to be playing for revenge—to make up for what happened last year. As long as I have anything to say about it, the answer will be "No way!" When you become vindictive, then vindictiveness becomes your focus, and that's not going to get the job done. All you'll have are more problems, more things to be vindictive about.

Vengeance just gets in the way and clouds up what you're doing. As a motivation it's highly overrated. That kind of motivation is going to last about as long as the first couple of hits. I've seen it happen so many times. I've seen people get so cranked up about what somebody said, or what somebody did the last time they played, or about what somebody said they're going to do this time, that that's all they think about. It's hard to play football that way for very long. If that's what's driving you, it's hard to concentrate on the task at hand.

The past is the past. Dwelling on it won't get you anywhere. It will only keep you in the past. When we're getting ready to play Utah or the Aggies or whoever, I don't say, "Remember last year." If it's someone that beat us the last time out, I don't say, "Let's get even." I don't carry grudges and I never will. There are people we've played who have done things I haven't liked very much. There are people we've played who have bugged me. Not many, but a few. I'm not oblivious to what is said and written. I'm human. But I know that to dwell on the negatives and to take any of it personally will only cloud my judgment and cause me to do things for the wrong reasons.

Playing the game is hard enough as it is without piling on some added cause. If on game day your primary focus isn't on your own preparation, then you're looking at a long afternoon. You can't be worrying about what kind of guy is lining up across from you, or what he said, or what he did to you last season. Your concentration needs to be on what to do if this happens, or if that happens. You need to play a football game, not a mind game.

Work on your own character, not someone else's.

We've won a good number of close games over the years, and I think one of the reasons we've been able to do that is that we've never really entered into the vengeance market. Of the sixteen WAC championships we've won, most have come down to the last game of the year when we've had to win or at least tie. I'm convinced that we've been successful a good share of the time because in large measure we've stayed focused on our own agenda and not on somebody else's. That's been especially true as we've added more success and have developed into the team everybody in the league points at. From Honolulu to El Paso, the game with BYU is the biggest game of the season. There's always a lot of motivation for the other team. Over the years we've gotten used to it and we've been able to live with it. If we were to get caught up in everything that's said and all the emotions and feelings going on, it would be difficult for us to play football and sustain any kind of success.

Beyond that, vengeance is no fun. Taking things personally is tough duty, and self-inflicted at that. It makes me tired just looking at someone whose agenda is full of getting even and answering back and getting revenge. I'm convinced that the key to being happy in anything you're doing—whether it's your relationship with your spouse or a co-worker, or your duties at work, or handling a leadership capacity, or whatever else—is to work through your tasks without taking personally the things that happen, without being easily offended. Only then can you focus on the job at hand and not cloud it over by some other agenda and motivation. Only then can you enjoy successful relationships.

My experience is that what you give, you get back. During my career I really haven't had to deal with a lot of conflict from other coaches. But, then, I haven't tried to drum any up, either.

When we played Michigan in the 1984 Holiday Bowl, Bo Schembechler, Michigan's head coach at the time, was quite outspoken about the blocking tactics of our offensive line. He made a number of disparaging remarks about what he thought was "legalized holding" by our linemen. To say the least, Bo did not come off as BYU's number one fan. He quickly became "the enemy."

But I maintained a cordial relationship with Bo at the press conferences leading up to the game, and after the game (which we won) as well. There were people who couldn't understand how I could do that. After what he said about our program, how could I continue to carry on with him like he was a friend?

Well, he was a friend, and he still is a friend, and all I had to do in that situation was separate the competition from the friendship. If I had chosen to take personally something that wasn't, I'm sure I could be involved in a feud with Bo Schembechler to this day. But I didn't choose to do that—and, for that matter, neither did he. I liked Bo before we played that game in 1984, and I've liked him ever since.

I'm not a good loser. I hate to get beaten—as much or more than anybody I know. Worse than that, I hate to not play well. Often I'm not very happy even after we've won a game—if we haven't played well. But I don't choose to lay the blame for our not playing well on the guy across the field, or to hold anything against him for doing everything he can to beat me.

I've built up a tremendous amount of respect for the job that coach across the field has to do, because it's the same job I have to do. My preference is to get along with that coach. In the Utah series, despite all the intensity associated with that rivalry over the years, I've been able to not only get along but to genuinely like virtually everybody they've had coaching for them. I've respected and liked them all. I know that's probably maddening to a lot of Utah and BYU fans, but it's the way I am and the way I prefer to be.

Coaches—and players for that matter—are extremely competitive by nature. If they weren't, they either wouldn't be in the game or they wouldn't last very long. I think that's important to keep in mind when you step into the arena. That understanding can put most things that happen in the heat of games, and seasons, in the proper perspective.

Winning is always going to generate more attention and, along with that, more criticism. Our 1984 national championship season was a good example of that. One of our most vocal critics was Oklahoma coach Barry Switzer, now the head coach of the Dallas Cowboys. Barry had a vested interest in how the end of the season polling went, of course, since his Sooners were next in line to BYU in the polls, so he was happy to comment on our schedule whenever he was asked—and sometimes when he wasn't asked. He said we didn't deserve to be Number 1 because the teams we played hadn't been of high enough caliber, and so on.

And why not? If he wanted Oklahoma to be Number 1, he had no other option than to try to persuade the voters to look past our undefeated record. I wasn't personally bothered at all by what he said about our schedule. I just hoped the voters wouldn't listen to him. I had a great deal of respect for Barry as a person and as a coach, and I felt the feeling was mutual. When the final polls came in, and we were voted Number 1, he sent me a note that I still have. "Congratulations," it said, along with a few other things that wouldn't get past the censor. Privately, he was perfectly capable of maintaining a good relationship with the "enemy" in Provo. Barry Switzer was a good example of not taking things personally.

A thin skin in this business is like a jail sentence. So is a long memory. Texas A&M beat us up pretty badly in the Holiday Bowl one year, 65–14, and ever since people have asked me what we'll do if we ever play them again. Well, if it's up to me we won't do anything differently. That game is over. They played their game and we played ours.

(I remember watching that Texas A&M team during warmups and thinking that I'd never been on a field—other than at Notre Dame— where I'd seen more great athletes. They passed the eyeball test, no question. Glen Tuckett walked by; and we were both looking at this player, number 33, who was quick and had size and speed. I said to Glen, "and that guy's not even playing.")

DEALING WITH THE MEDIA

So many things have to roll off your back. If you let them stick, pretty soon you're carrying quite a load. A couple of years ago the season was about to start when *Sports Illustrated* came out with a cover story that declared BYU the most hated football team in America. BYU the most hated football team in America? Maybe the most hated team in the Rocky Mountains, but America? I didn't see how we could compete with Notre Dame.

That issue brought all kinds of letters to the editor, many with Provo postmarks. Some people really got incensed. This was an open invitation to take it personally, and a lot of people did just that. As a result, the magazine got what it wanted: a lot of controversy—and, I presume, a lot of sales. In its own way, it was also just playing the game.

The media is a business too, and it's important not to lose sight of that. Most of what's written or what's said isn't personal, and even if some of it is personal, there's no percentage in paying any attention to it.

I got my best tip on dealing with the media during my first year of high school coaching. We'd started out with a couple of wins and already the papers were saying some good things about us. Granite High School had been in kind of a slump for a few years, and this was being heralded as the end of that. Then we lost and suddenly the newspapers didn't carry such an optimistic tone. I was allowing myself to get worked up over what I saw as unfair reporting when Bill Coltrin, a sports writer for the *Salt Lake Tribune,* came by practice one afternoon. I said something to Bill, who was a great friend over the years, about wanting to set the record straight—and I've never forgotten the advice he gave me. He said, "Be careful about how much spouting off you do, even if you're right. They go to press 365 days a year. You'll have your one day in the sun, but they'll have their 365."

I've tried to keep the media in that perspective ever since. I like sports and I like to read the newspapers and listen to sportscasts. But for my own good there are some things I don't choose to read or listen to. The sports media has changed over the years, with more and more controversy in the headlines. The biggest change has been in the sports talk shows. They've got to fill twenty-four hours a day, some of them, and they're not going to fill it and be very interesting without creating controversy.

I could be a lot more controversial than I am, and I suppose in some ways I could be friendlier with the press. But I've always been conscious of who I work for, and I let that restrain me because I know I should. I've always been quite measured in the things I say. Sometimes I'd like to say more, but I think about my duty as a coach, both to BYU and to what BYU represents.

I've never tried to manipulate the media. I don't plant stories, and I don't give background off the record. Many things that become public would never see the light of print if it were my call. I'd never personally make a press release about kids quitting the squad or about internal disciplinary actions, for instance. I don't see where that does anybody any good. I'm not arguing the pros and cons of the first amendment or the public's right to know. I'm just saying that if it's my choice, I don't publicize those kinds of things.

I'm not oblivious to what people in the media say and do, but I'm not going to let it affect the way I do things—whether the commentary is positive or negative. I work hard at that. If I get nailed by some sports writer about the way I coached on Saturday, I can hear it and then forget about it. I can see the writer the next day and carry on without a grudge.

If I start an article and I don't like it, I won't read it. I'll just stop reading. That seems to be such a simple solution to me. If someone's trying to stir up controversy, I don't want to feed into it. I don't want to be a part of it. During the past few seasons a newsletter has circulated around Utah Valley that quotes some "secret informant" inside the football program. People ask me who I think the informant is. I say I don't know and I don't care. I'm really not interested. You can get so many hang-ups in this business if you allow it; you can become so paranoid you can't function.

There are times when the program deserves to be taken to task. I don't have a problem with that. And there have been plenty of positive media features done on our program. I certainly don't have a problem with that, either. The media is going to cut both ways. The key, again, is in not taking things personally.

IT'S NOT NUCLEAR SCIENCE

It's always helpful, too, to remember that the subject is college football, not germ warfare or nuclear science. It's a game, after all, and the reason we play it, and watch it, is to enjoy ourselves. There is so much amusement and humor in the game that it's a shame if any of it gets lost by taking things too seriously.

To me, a sense of humor is vital in all aspects of life, especially in major college football. If any young coach were to ask me what he needed to survive and thrive in the business, I'd tell him he should start with a sense of humor. Humor can not only get you through some tough times, but sometimes it will even let you enjoy them.

No matter how dire the circumstance, a little humor can go a long way in defusing it.

Take, for example, that story about BYU being America's most hated football team. A lot of people saw no humor at all in that story, and I have to admit at first glance I thought it was pretty preposterous and I myself didn't find the prospect all that funny. But then I thought about it and saw the humor in the very fact that it was preposterous. When I was asked for my reaction all I said was, "Well, I was here when we were the most loved team in America, when we were number one on everybody's homecoming list, and personally I'd take what we have now."

I appreciate a sense of humor in others. I think it's an effective way to communicate, and there's always a semblance of truth in humor. My daughter, Ann, has a great sense of humor. She and her family generally come to the house in Provo after our home games. She has five kids. I'll say to her, "I'm really glad when you come and I can see the family, and I'm really glad when you leave," and she'll just laugh. She knows what I mean.

Humor runs in the family. My father had a great sense of humor. He loved jokes. One of my earliest boyhood memories is me standing next to my dad working in the field and me peppering him with question after question, the way kids will do. He was working and wasn't paying much attention. All he'd say was "I don't know," or he wouldn't answer at all. Then finally, after five or six questions, he stopped working and started laughing. "This reminds me of the story about the guy whose boy kept asking him questions and the father kept saying he didn't know the answer," he said to me. "The boy said, 'Dad, do you mind me asking you these questions?' And the dad said, 'No, I don't mind. How else are you going to learn?'"

My dad was like that. He'd stop in the middle of what he was doing and tell some story or joke. He'd tell me about the farmer who won a million dollars in the lottery and when they asked him what he was going to do with the money he said, "Well, I guess I'll just keep farming until it's gone."

I like spontaneous humor. My wife, Patti, has a knack for great timing. After we'd won the national championship in 1984, *Sports Illustrated* did a big article on the program. I was looking through it at home one night and read the writer's description of me, which went something like "The Cougars are coached by LaVell Edwards, a rather large, lumpy chap, a bit of a poet and a romantic." I didn't quite understand what that meant. Patti was sitting there and I read it to her and asked her what she thought it meant.

Without looking up or missing a beat she said, "It means you're a fat daydreamer."

Humor has kept me loose over the years and helped me to not get too bogged down by the pressures and the criticisms that come with the business. I like seeing most things in the most humorous light possible. As I've said, there's usually a semblance of truth in anything humorous. Sometimes making fun of yourself can be the healthiest thing you can do. It helps you avoid taking yourself too seriously, and it allows you to agree with your critics in a way that can often disarm them.

When there was a lot of grumbling a couple of years ago about the missionary program giving us an advantage with older players, for example, I was asked about our prospects for the upcoming season and I said, "This is the youngest football team we've had in a number of years. . . . We average only twenty-five years of age." A lot of people picked up on that quote around the country and I think it was good for the program. If you can poke fun at yourself, it takes the edge off.

Humor is great that way. It smooths feelings. It puts things in an enjoyable light. A few years ago, when I said, "I'd rather lose and live in Provo than win and live in Laramie," it was exaggerated enough that it turned out to be a lot of fun. One of the radio stations in Laramie called me and asked if I'd do a promo for our game against Wyoming the next season. I said, "Hi, I'm LaVell Edwards, please come to Laramie, Wyoming, my very favorite place, to see Wyoming play BYU." That wound up being broadcast all around the state, and the stadium was sold out when we played there. What I said ended up selling a lot of seats, and, semblance of truth or not, because I said it the way I did, they never even asked me to take it back.

*Dick MacPherson,
retired college and pro coach*

"The World's Most Famous Mormon"

They couldn't have *given* Dick MacPherson the job. They could have offered him a membership in the country club, a new Cadillac, and a driver to drive it. They could have offered him the Tabernacle Choir, and he'd have turned them down. And he wasn't the only one.

"BYU wasn't going to make it, that was a well-known fact," says MacPherson, who won over one hundred games coaching football at Massachusetts and Syracuse before he retired in 1990. "Everybody in coaching knew it. I was at the University of Massachusetts when Hal Kopp went to BYU from Rhode Island. Hal was a great football coach, but he didn't know what he was getting into and he didn't last.

"Their priorities just weren't there. If you're going to be successful at a school the number one priority has to be football, and it was obvious that at BYU the number one priority was God, and a close number two was family. I mean, all of us preach it—God, family, and then profession, but how many of us live it?

"Then they found a guy who lived it. LaVell Edwards took a job that was not doable and he did it.

"People say that coaching is coaching, that

it's the same wherever you go. But coaching is not the same. It's different, because the priorities and needs of people are different. You have to coach differently in one place than you do in another. You have to adapt. LaVell understood that. He understood the priorities of Brigham Young University, the Mormons, and Provo, Utah. He showed us all that coaching *is* different.

"There's really no success story like his. No one saw it coming. His background is lineman and single wing, and he becomes the pass-happy genius of America at a coaching graveyard. And he keeps winning when he's not supposed to. Year in, year out, you don't see BYU on the top twenty-five national recruiting charts. And yet year in, year out, they're among the nation's top twenty-five teams.

"Every coach out there knows who he is and what he's done. They know he did the impossible. He's inspired coaches from all walks of life—by the way he adapts, by the way he handles people, by the way he lives, by the way he gets along. He makes people feel comfortable being around him, which is a great compliment to his faith. If he's a Mormon, maybe we all should be.

"I happen to think he's the world's most famous Mormon, by the way, which is a point I happened to make once when I was playing golf at the Doral Open Pro-Am in Florida. I was in a group with Tony Burns, the president of Ryder Trucks, one of the tournament sponsors. Tony's a Mormon, and I told him of being in Salt Lake City the previous Christmas with LaVell. We'd gone to the Tabernacle to hear the choir, and when he walked in the crowd really started buzzing. All through the building there was this awareness that LaVell was there, the coach was there, in the Tabernacle. I told Tony, 'You know, this guy is bigger than the leaders of the Mormon Church.' Well, right next to Tony *was* one of the leaders of the Mormon Church. I turned to him and said, 'That proves my point. I don't know who you are.'"

One of the most intriguing things to me about where BYU has managed to go these past twenty-plus years is that so many of the stops have been unscheduled. When we sat down in 1972 and made an effort to stop looking at all the reasons we couldn't win and instead tried to put a positive spin on all the reasons we could, no one suggested we become the new Notre Dame. The new BYU would be fine by us.

In no one's wildest imagination—at least no one's imagination that I knew of—were there dreams of a national championship. There was no master plan to win Heisman trophies, Outland trophies, national coach of the year awards, a succession of All-American quarterbacks, hundreds of NCAA passing and total offense records, graduates from the program who would play on thirteen straight Super Bowl winners—and probably least of all, no dreams of going to a bowl game at the end of every season. In 1972 the school hadn't been to even one bowl—in history.

We didn't give any thought to how many games we might win in ten years or twenty years (although we did give the occasional thought to where we might *be* in ten years or twenty years). I never knew there was a hundred-win club or a two hundred–win club for coaches, and I certainly would never have thought about trying to join them.

We did set out to win the league every year, but even then, we didn't think about winning it more than one year in a row. Nobody said, "Let's win sixteen titles in twenty years."

CHAPTER TEN

Trophies

Looking back at twenty-plus seasons that have produced all of the above, and more, it's almost frightening to consider the list. And it *is* frightening—at least it is to me—to think of what might happen if you set out from day one actually trying to accomplish all of the above. If you started out requiring those kinds of things of yourself and of your program, you'd probably drive yourself right out of coaching and right into therapy. There's a reason coaches like to take things one game at a time. It's spelled s-a-n-i-t-y.

Not only are you better off not dwelling on the future because of the pressure you're able to avoid, but, even more important, you're better off when your sights aren't set on the honors and the laurels—some call them spoils—that come with victory.

If you set your sights on these by-products, it's easy to lose sight of your real objective, which is to play the best football, with the best attitude, that you possibly can.

There's a big difference between expecting to be successful and expecting to win the Heisman Trophy.

When you expect to be successful, it follows that you'll plan ahead, you'll prepare yourself, you'll make certain that you follow all the steps that have helped you be successful in the past, or you've watched others who have found success. When opportunity presents itself, you'll be in a position to open the door. That's your focus. That's your game plan.

But when your expectation is that you'll win the Heisman Trophy, then you're focusing on an outgrowth of success—a symptom, really—and that can change your focus. Instead of concentrating on being prepared, you'll tend to concentrate more on where you stand in the race, and how far ahead or behind schedule you might be. You'll worry more. You'll keep an eye on how your competition is doing. You'll wonder if you have a good enough promotion department. You'll worry whether your statistics are strong enough. You'll still work hard and practice hard, no doubt, but you'll have a lot more distractions, and most of them won't be good distractions. It will be much harder to focus.

When your focus is on your own preparation you have total control, but when your focus is on the prize, you in fact have very little control.

You can control how hard you practice, how long you lift weights, how much time you spend in the film room, how hard you're going to play on Saturday. All those things are under your own command.

But you *can't* control how the other guy is going to play on Saturday, you can't manipulate statistics, to a large extent you can't control public relations, and you can't vote in the Heisman Trophy balloting. Those things are all up to somebody else.

Worrying about what somebody else is doing—be it a player, a coach, a voter, a sports information director, whoever—will only heighten your anxiety and slowly but surely turn you from a team-oriented football player into one with an individual focus.

That might work for a tennis player, but in the sport of football, it doesn't.

TEAM SUCCESS BRINGS INDIVIDUAL SUCCESS

We tell our players this all the time. The more success the team has, the more individual recognition will come their way. There are certain outgrowths of team play that will just happen. Trust in that, not in yourself. Play hard for the team, not for individual honors. If we all collectively work at it and do our best, then as an outgrowth of that we're going to have All-Americans, we're going to have people in the race for the Heisman.

The important thing is that you don't focus on your own goals and ambitions, but you focus on the team.

The same applies to the goal of playing pro football. If you come into a program with that as your goal, it can deter you from thinking of the team first. It's only when you think of the team first that you start to realize your own true potential. If you want to be a pro, team play is by far the best way to get there.

That's one of the reasons we don't have a shrine, so to speak, in the football office displaying this trophy or that trophy. We do have a replica of the Heisman Trophy in the foyer, and we have a variety of trophies we've won over the years on display here and there. But there never has been a desire to put the trophies ahead of the program. If I stop to think about it—which I generally don't—I'd have to say that the haphazard way the trophies are displayed reflects the approach we've had over the years to obtaining them. They are merely the souvenirs collected along the journey and not the journey itself.

They are what happened along the way of trying to get better.

Not that they aren't appreciated. Whether they're gathering dust in a corner or they're under a two thousand–watt spotlight, over time the trophies do reflect the direction of your program. They reflect a team effort. Again using the Heisman Trophy as an example, even though it is deemed the highest individual honor in college football, it is actually far from an individual award. In the first place, you're not going to win it unless you're on a successful team—at least nobody has yet. And beyond that, the award's history clearly suggests that one of the prerequisites to winning the trophy is to come from a consistently successful program.

When Ty Detmer won the Heisman Trophy in 1990, it had as much to do with Gary Sheide and Gifford Nielsen and Marc Wilson and Jim McMahon and Steve Young and Robbie Bosco as it did with Ty Detmer. All those quarterbacks who came before Ty, who placed seventh or fifth or third or second in the Heisman voting, helped pave the way. Having all of them continually involved in the Heisman race did nothing but increase BYU's credibility over the years. When Ty came along and he had a big junior season, one that included a win over Miami in early September, he was able to stand on the shoulders of all those BYU quarterbacks who came before him.

It's the same with any individual honors that have come my way. Without the entire program supporting me, I'd never have gotten any of them. My coaching staff, my players, the BYU administration, my family, the people who fill the seats every Saturday—they've all played a big role in any recognition that has come to me. And I've always tried to keep things in that perspective. I couldn't have gotten to one hundred wins, and then to two hundred wins, without plenty of help. I couldn't have gotten to ten wins.

That's why it's never bothered me when others in the program get recognition. A lot of our coaches have received some very good job offers over the years. That's a high compliment in our business, and I think one that reflects favorably on the program they're coming from. It's always made me feel good to think we were smart enough to recognize the ability in a coach, which is why he was hired in the first place.

To me, the hardest part about success is trying to keep it going. It was John Wooden, the great UCLA basketball coach, who summed it up best when he said, "Getting to the top of the mountain isn't the hard part. Staying there is."

Whatever you might decide is the top of the mountain, once you've arrived at that level of success the pressure of staying there is unavoidably going to increase. I believe that's inevitable. Just as the Heismans and the Outlands and the championships increase with your success, so does the pressure. It simply comes with the territory. If you're going to be successful, pressure is going to come along for the ride.

It's impossible to be oblivious to that kind of pressure. But I don't believe it's impossible to control it. You can choose how you want to look at it, and you can choose to not let it be consuming.

A long time ago I came to the conclusion that there are only a certain number of things I can do. As a football coach, I can prepare my players, I can formulate a game plan, and I can assemble the best staff possible. Beyond that I'm into areas I either have no control over, or I have limited control at best; and if I'm smart, I'm careful about how much I let those areas affect me and what I do. A high level of consistency is going to come only if I take care of my own business, of those things I have control over.

I've always had such great respect for Tom Osborne and the program he runs at the University of Nebraska because that's what Tom does—he tends to his own business. Year in, year out, Nebraska is there, playing hard and having success. They move to the beat of their own drum, so to speak, and they just keep going. It impresses me even more when I note that Nebraska doesn't do it with the most talented teams in the world. You almost never see Nebraska in the top ten on the national recruiting lists that come out every spring. It's a fact that they don't get the most prized recruits to come to Lincoln. And yet they've averaged about ten wins a year for as long as I can remember. I think they've done a remarkable job.

When you're consistent, you're going to get recognition. Maybe it's not exactly when and where everyone would like, but over the long run you're going to be as consistently recognized as your program is consistent.

It's curious to me that people will ask me if it bothers me that BYU doesn't get more recognition. I don't understand that. I think, What more recognition do you want? We went 6 and 6 in 1993, and when the preseason polls came out for 1994 almost every one of them had us ranked in the top twenty-five again. To me, that's recognition. It's recognition that you've been consistent. I can remember the days when BYU would finally make it to the top twenty—and then be dropped forever (it seemed) for losing just one game, and that maybe by only one point. Yet in 1993 we lost six games and didn't drop out. I haven't felt a lack of recognition or respect over the years. Instead, I've felt just the opposite.

I continue to be amazed that we've received the recognition we have, and I suspect I always will be. To have as much national attention as has been directed toward the football stadium located just a mile or two from the farm where I was born and raised—that will always be a source of astonishment to me.

Heaven knows I've got little to complain about. I've been flattered enough. I've been able to hold down a steady job, I've had my share of individual recognition, the teams I've been a part of have enjoyed success, and I've had other people occasionally interested in my services.

PRO FOOTBALL AND OTHER TEMPTATIONS

I came close to leaving BYU only once. And that wasn't as close as I led myself—and the Detroit Lions—to believe at the time.

It was in 1984, just after we'd gone 13–0 in the regular season and had won the national championship. I got a call from a scout for the Lions I'd known for years named Jerry Neary. He wanted to know if I'd have any interest in the Detroit job.

I told him if they wanted to talk, I'd listen. I'd had a number of job offers to that point in my career, most of them from college teams and one or two feelers from the United States Football League, a professional league at the time. But I'd made up my mind I didn't want to leave BYU for the USFL or for any other college job.

The only way I'd leave Provo, I'd decided, was to coach in the National Football League. That appealed to me for a number of reasons. I'd coached in the service, I'd coached in high school, and I'd coached in college. There was only one step left on the ladder. I wondered what it would be like to coach in the pros, and I also was curious to know if some of the things that worked at BYU could work in the NFL.

When the Lions got back to me they said they wanted to get together right away. I told them I'd be coaching in the East-West game in San Francisco. They said they'd contact me there. But I was there all week and nothing happened. In the meantime, as I understand it, they were negotiating with Chuck Knox to see if he wanted the job, and he eventually turned them down.

From San Francisco I went to Nashville for the college football coaching convention. It was there that the Lions caught up with me again. I talked to Russ Thomas, their general manager, and he asked if I could fly immediately to Detroit to meet with them. I told him I'd love to but I was on the board of trustees at the convention, I was going to receive the Coach of the Year award at the banquet the next night, and then I had to go to Washington, D.C., to meet President Ronald Reagan in the White House on Friday. I know—excuses, excuses. But I told him I really couldn't fly to Detroit right then.

He asked me what time I was flying in to Washington. I told him it would be in the morning, about three hours before the meeting with the president was scheduled. He said fine, he'd meet me at the airport, which he did.

He'd booked a room at the airport Marriott for our meeting, and we talked there for a couple of hours. He said I was the coach they wanted and wondered if I could reroute my trip home so I could stop in Detroit and work out the details. Again I told him I'd like to but I couldn't. We had a big recruiting group coming in that weekend to Provo, they'd be at the basketball game on Saturday night, and I really needed to be there. He said he understood, so I flew to Provo and took care of that. On Sunday night Mr. Ford, the owner of the club, called me at home. He told me the job was mine and all we needed to do was sign the papers. I said, "Fine, just let me have a day." I'd try to have everything straightened away at BYU the next day, Monday, and I'd get back to him Monday night.

Sometime between a sleepless Sunday night and Monday morning it dawned on me: My heart just wasn't in this decision. If I wasn't willing to drop everything and go, what business did I have going at all?

I called them back and said I'd changed my mind; I'd decided to stay at BYU. They were gracious about it, and they went to work on getting someone else. Within a week they hired Darryl Rodgers. I remember reading about it in the paper and getting kind of an empty feeling—wondering if I'd done the right thing. I'd turned down a job in the NFL that was now Darryl's, and the paper said he'd signed for something like $250,000 a year, which was a lot of money then (and now). We'd never gotten around to talking salary, but I'm sure the money would have been the same for me.

As it turned out, things didn't go too well for Darryl and the Lions in the next few seasons. Billy Sims, their great running back, hurt his knee, and while he came back, he never did come back to his previous form. They'd drafted a quarterback high in the draft and that didn't work out either. Darryl was fired and went into athletic administration for a while. He was a good coach and a capable administrator and didn't have trouble finding jobs after Detroit, but he had to move around a lot.

It was an offer from the University of Minnesota earlier in the '80s that helped me make up my mind that I would discourage any feelers from other colleges. At the end of almost every season I would talk to schools about jobs, usually on behalf of assistants who were looking to move up as head coaches, and often I would find myself in a position of having to say whether I was personally interested in the job. In the case of Minnesota—and I have to give them credit for their aggressiveness— they flew representatives out in a private jet to Provo just to talk, and for every reason I gave that it wouldn't be best for me to move, they countered it with a compelling reason why I should leave. Something in me sensed that I was really only leading them on, that I didn't want to ever leave BYU for another college, and I should finally admit that to myself. So I did just that. After that, I didn't even "talk" about other jobs.

Probably the most intriguing job feeler I ever got—in the context of what's happened since—was in 1976 from the University of Miami. We were playing in the Tangerine Bowl that year in Orlando, Florida, and John Green, who was then the vice-president at Miami, called and asked if he and Pete Elliott, the athletic director, could drive up from Miami and take me to dinner. When we met they asked if I had any interest in being a part of a new direction for the football program at Miami. They said football was at a crossroads in Miami. They hadn't had much success of late, attendance was falling, and it was time to either get it right and be successful or give up the sport entirely. They talked about paying enough money to be a strong incentive to a prospective head coach. The salary would be $75,000 a year for five years. At the time that seemed like all the money in the world.

They weren't making an offer. They just wanted to talk and feel out my interest. The next day, things got a little more public than either of us planned, and it was my fault. I was playing golf with Larry Guest, the sports editor of the Orlando paper, and I asked him what his thoughts were about the Miami situation. I mentioned to him that I had had dinner with the people from Miami and that they were prepared to pay someone $75,000 a year. The next morning's newspaper had a story with the headline: "Edwards Offered Five-Year, $375,000 Deal." Obviously Larry had been writing down what I'd said, even though I hadn't been paying attention.

There were too many things about the Miami situation that

bothered me. Probably the biggest one was that Miami wasn't in Provo. And it was unsettling that they might jerk the rug out if the program didn't go in the right direction. I didn't pursue them any more and they didn't pursue me. They ended up hiring Lou Saban, a veteran coach who'd been in the NFL and had a lot of experience and who wound up doing a great job. I honestly don't know if I had either enough experience or the right background to be able to do what Lou did. He was really the guy who got them going. He was like a Larry Brown in basketball—someone just offbeat enough to come in, have great success, and then move on. Howard Schnellenberger came in after Lou, and he got Jim Kelly for his quarterback. Then Jimmy Johnson came along. And then Dennis Erickson. The last I heard, they still hadn't dropped football at Miami.

When I came home after playing the Tangerine Bowl, a copy of the story in the *Orlando Sentinel* had preceded me. I got a call from Ben Lewis, the vice-president of BYU in charge of athletics at the time. He said he wanted to talk, so we met for lunch and he pulled out the article. He looked at me and said, "Let's talk about this. But before we do you might as well know up front that you're not going anywhere."

I've laughed about that many times since—President Lewis making it clear that I wasn't going anywhere else. I think I did get a little bit of a pay raise out of that experience, but the best thing I got was that good feeling that comes from being wanted. When they don't want you to leave, you must be doing something right.

Living with the Media

Patti Edwards

Normally when you're a football coach you try to keep a comfortable distance from the press.

But then normally your wife isn't a sports writer.

When Patti Edwards took a job as a column writer for the *Provo Daily Herald*, LaVell Edwards, the head football coach at BYU, found himself living with the media.

"He had no choice," says Patti Edwards, journalist, who wrote her *Daily Herald* sports column off and on for more than a decade. "He couldn't avoid me. I was always there."

Marriages have run aground for less.

"But you know what, he never once tried to tell me what I should write or what I shouldn't write," says Patti.

Sure, he turned his paycheck over to her every month—but it wasn't because he wanted good copy.

"It was something I wanted to do and this was a great outlet," says Patti. "It didn't pay that much, but I got to write."

Most of the time she wrote about Cougar football. She wrote about the team. She wrote about players on the team. She wrote about her husband. Sometimes she would get controversial. Sometimes she would take a stand. Always she presented her own words, her own ideas.

"It wasn't that LaVell couldn't have manipulated me," she goes on. "I mean, he can do that. He can be good at it. I remember when the kids were little and we had this old Volkswagen. He had them all convinced that that car had flubber gear and it could fly. They'd get in it, and he'd tell them to close their eyes because that's the only way the car could get airborne. Then as they drove around town he would describe how everything looked from the air. He'd say, 'Look, there's John's friend's house. Look, there's Utah Lake.' But they couldn't open their eyes or the car would crash.

"They flew around Provo all summer. They were always bugging him to go for a plane ride. LaVell said he didn't know quite what to think of his kids' intelligence. I mean, they were *buying it.*"

But she digresses.

"Me writing that column was just never an issue," she says. "It was just one of the things I did."

Her husband the coach never interfered, other than the time he took several writing awards Patti had won and had them framed so she could hang them on the wall above her desk.

"He was more proud of those awards than I was," says Patti.

"He's always been one to notice what anyone in the family is doing and to recognize it. He is very aware. I'm sure he could buy my clothes better for me than I could. He's never bought me anything I've taken back. I remember one time when I'd been to this big sale and I was all excited about this suit I'd bought for practically nothing. I showed it to LaVell and he said, 'Well, it looks fine, except the lapels might be too big. Probably why it was on sale,' he said. He was right. The lapels were out of style. I hadn't even noticed."

But again she digresses.

"The great part about writing that column was that it gave me an opportunity to do something on my own and he could support me in it," she says. "Just as I could support him in what he was doing. It was good for me. It gave me a lot of self-confidence."

And there was never any editing? Never any critical comment?

"Never," Patti insists, "although there was this one time that I wrote this column that I really liked and I said to LaVell, 'This is so good it makes me want to cry' and he said, 'It makes me want to cry too.'"

CHAPTER ELEVEN

Beliefs

I was once asked, prior to a game BYU was playing against another school with religious ties, "Don't you think God wants you to win?"

My answer was that when it comes to the outcome of a football game, I really don't think God has a preference.

I have a strong personal belief in a Father in Heaven. I believe he helps me when I ask for help, and, yes, I think that means helping me coach football games. But I believe he'll also help the other side. I'm sure he really enjoys the game. How could he not enjoy seeing people utilize the talents he gave them and trying their very best? But I'm sure the scoreboard is not his concern at all. I'm sure he doesn't even look at the final score. His interest isn't in the outcome but in the process. We pray before and after every game we play, but our prayers are for strength, for endurance, for safety, and for the ability to play our best.

While I don't presume to know all of Heavenly Father's ways and reasons, I do strongly believe he is aware of all that we do, as his children, and that as a loving Father his desire is that we live righteously. To that end, he wants us to help each other grow and develop—together. I believe that he puts us in various places and gives us circumstances that give us opportunities to help and serve one other. Whether or not we choose to take advantage of those opportunities is up to us. That's a decision we each have to make individually.

My family had a great deal to do with the shaping of my personal beliefs, of course, and I was fortunate to come from a very large and what I consider a very great family that made it easier for me to have the faith I do. My father was a Church leader in any number of capacities, a man devoid of hypocrisy. My brothers and sisters live God-fearing lives that have always been, and continue to be, great examples to me. But despite all that, it's remained for me to make my own decisions about what kind of life I'm going to live, and how much a belief in God is going to be a part of it.

FINDING MY OWN INDIVIDUALITY

The more I study the gospel of Jesus Christ, the more I've come to appreciate that individuality. I believe Jesus taught that we are each accountable for our own decisions and resolutions as well as our own talents. We have to gain our own faith, our own testimony. We can get tremendous input from others—the way my family gave me tremendous input—but ultimately we're each responsible for our own lives. In the gospel we're individuals first. Our Father in Heaven can do anything, but he won't live our lives for us, and he won't let anyone else live them for us either.

When Patti and I were just starting our own family we had to make a conscious decision for ourselves just how much of an influence religion would have in our lives. I remember right after we had our first child, Ann, we sat down and had quite a lengthy discussion about how active we wanted to be in the Church and what kinds of standards we wanted in our home.

Fortunately, Patti and I were of a similar mind, and our goals and desires were compatible. I have thought many times since just how important it is to have a marriage partner who has the same beliefs and desires as you do. I guess in a way Patti and I were lucky, because while we were dating we didn't really talk about such things that much. But I think deep down we both knew enough about each other that we knew how the other felt. I think we both understood that when it came time to get serious about it, we would be of a similar mind.

Our conscious determination that we'd let the Church and the gospel be prominent in our home meant that we'd be willing to serve our Father in Heaven in whatever ways he wanted us to. Once you make that decision, you leave it up to the Lord, accepting that his ways aren't always going to coincide with what you had previously thought.

One of the bigger surprises of my life was being called to be a bishop. For some reason I'd never perceived of myself as a bishop. My perception was that a bishop was a man who was very knowledgeable in the gospel, who had all the right answers, who was an excellent speaker, and who didn't make any mistakes. I knew I was incapable of that. I did not fit that profile.

But no more than a week after I came to BYU as an assistant coach in the fall of 1962, I was called to be bishop of the BYU 36th Ward, a student ward on campus. I accepted the call warily, to say the least.

But it wasn't long after I moved into that calling and started to counsel and talk with the young people of that ward that the realization struck me that I wasn't called to be a bishop because of some superior spirituality I had, or because I was extremely righteous. I was called to be a bishop of that ward at that time because of what I personally had to offer. My personality or my approach could be used to make a specific connection with some of the people in that ward who needed it. In my own way I could help someone else. There might be those who would have to wait for someone else who would be just right for them. But there were also those whom I could help right then. I was a bishop because of what I had to offer. It meant I could fulfill my calling without having to be perfect. Which was a very good thing.

Those first years at BYU were some of the toughest times our family ever had. Ann developed nephritis and had to stay in bed for much of the first year we were in Provo. Patti was pregnant with Jimmy, and after he was born there were some medical complications she had to deal with. We'd just moved, I was starting a new job, and on top of that I was a new bishop. It was really a very hectic, very demanding time in our lives. But looking back, it was also very rewarding. In many ways it helped shape us for the things to come.

That term as bishop had a profound effect in helping me see my own individuality. It made me more aware than I'd ever been that there were certain ways I did things that were unique to me, and they could be successful. I'm sure you couldn't have convinced me at the time that my term as bishop would also be invaluable training to become a head football coach. But it proved to be just that. So many of the things I did as a bishop would be the same things I would do later when I became BYU's head football coach. In many, many ways I haven't conducted myself any differently as a head coach than I conducted myself as the bishop of the BYU 36th Ward. In both, I've spent a lot of time talking individually with people, trying to get them to do things a little differently, and I guess better.

I've found that when you can be a positive influence in someone else's life, to whatever degree, it has a positive influence on your own life. It's unavoidable. What goes around comes around, in other words. Service is reciprocal. I know one of the reasons I enjoy coaching and working with athletes is that, just as was the case with those members of the 36th Ward, they inspire me so much.

A number of years ago I read a talk by Bob Richards, the great Olympic pole vaulter and motivational speaker, that describes the way I feel about athletes and their infectious thinking process. He talked about a writer in Oakland who was going to write an article about the great author Jack London. He had a quote from a story that Jack London had written, and he asked Kenny Stabler, the quarterback at the time for the Oakland Raiders, for a reaction. The quote went as follows:

I'd rather be ashes than dust. I'd rather my flame go out in a burning spark than to be stifled with dry rot. I'd rather be a splendid meteor blazing across the sky, every atom in me in magnificent glow, than be a sleepy and permanent planet. Life is to be lived, not to exist. I shall not waste my days trying to prolong them. I will use my time.

After reading that quote, the writer asked Kenny Stabler what he thought it meant.

He thought for a minute and said, "Throw deep."

I think that really cut to the heart of what Jack London was writing about; and it also cuts to the heart of an athlete's mentality. Whatever label we put on it, whether it's "Lengthen your stride," or "Go for broke," or "Throw deep," what we're really talking about is getting ourselves outside of that little safety area we have a tendency to want to stay within.

Kenny Stabler's reply typified the tendency all great athletes have to stretch themselves. They have that extra ability to think and go beyond the norm. I know that's been the case with the great quarterbacks we've had at BYU and with the other great athletes we've had in the program. They don't accept arbitrary limitations. They're not afraid to go beyond conventional thinking. Challenges, and the fear of failure, do not scare them off.

We'd never have been able to find success with a passing attack if we hadn't had people who were willing to look for greater possibilities and not merely listen to those who had already passed judgment.

LIMITATIONS AND POSSIBILITIES

I was thumbing through a magazine a few years ago when I saw an advertisement for a computer company that illustrated what I'm talking about. The ad had pictures of several people and quotes attributed to them. They included:

"Everything that can be invented has been invented."
—*Charles Duell, director of the United States Patent Office, 1899.*

"Who in the [world] wants to hear actors talk?"
—*Harry M. Warner, Warner Bros. Pictures, 1927.*

"Sensible and responsible women do not want to vote."
—*Grover Cleveland, 1905.*

"There is no likelihood man can ever tap the power of the atom."
—*Robert Millikan, Nobel Prize winner in physics, 1923.*

"Heavier than air flying machines are impossible."
—*Lord Kelvin, president of the Royal Society, 1895.*

"Ruth made a big mistake when he gave up pitching."
—*Tris Speaker, Hall of Fame baseball player, 1921.*

The ad went on to talk about the limitations people put upon themselves and others, and of course ended with a pitch to buy the company's computer, which could do things people wouldn't have dreamed of ten years before. The point was obvious. It's only when we close our minds that we shut ourselves off from our full potential. Being around people whose tendency is *not* to do that, who are always testing their limits, has been, and continues to be, an exhilarating experience for me.

I love the way an athlete's mind works; I love the thought processes; I love the intensity. I looked at Michael Jordan trying to make it in baseball and I thought, That's truly a great thing. After all he'd accomplished in basketball, after all the money he'd made, he was still driven by that athlete's instinct that makes him want to see what else he can do, how far he can go. Because of that he was willing to start at the bottom and ride in a bus again. Maybe he rode in an air-conditioned bus he bought with his own money, but he rode in that bus and he played in the minors—and it wasn't because there were any guarantees he'd be successful. He just wanted to see how far he could go.

And even though Michael Jordan wasn't as successful in baseball as he hoped to be, I suspect it was easier for him to deal with and accept than many of his fans. I don't say it didn't bother him. I think it may have bothered him a great deal. But he seemed able to *accept* it. (What was harder for him to accept, I think, was losing the chance to compete because of the baseball strike of 1994–95.) I think another attribute great athletes tend to share is the ability to take responsibility for their actions, good or bad, and recognize the difference between those things you can control and those things you can't.

Sean Covey had a profound impact on me in that regard. He was the kind of person who made his own decisions and determined his own actions, and he didn't let circumstances beyond his control dictate what he would do.

I'd known Sean since he was a young boy. He grew up just around the corner. I was his priests quorum adviser at church, and I knew his family very well. They're all outstanding people. His father is Stephen R. Covey, the motivational writer and speaker. I always joked that Sean had the "Seven Habits of Highly Effective People" memorized by the time he was ten. Everyone in the Covey family did.

Growing up, Sean was kind of a chubby kid. I didn't think much about him as an athlete until my son Jimmy came home from high school one day and said Sean Covey was going to be a great quarterback. He ended up starting for Provo High School as a sophomore and helped the school win the state championship when he was a senior. He was a 4.0 student and could have gone to a lot of colleges, but he chose BYU because he wanted to play quarterback and lead the school to a national championship. He wasn't bashful about it at all. That was what he envisioned. That was his goal.

He enrolled at BYU and played J.V. ball for us his first year. He had a great season. He was developing very well. After serving a mission for two years, he returned and threw himself back into his football goals more diligently than ever. We've probably had kids who worked as hard as Sean Covey, but we've never had anybody who's worked harder. He lifted, he ran, he threw, he studied, he worked at it. He did everything you're supposed to do to be successful as a football player.

It paid off about halfway through his sophomore year when we were struggling and he got a chance to play. We won most of the rest of our games that season with Sean as the starter. But the next year wasn't quite as successful. Sean had a concussion in the opener, and that was followed by other injuries, including a knee injury that was quite serious. When the season was over he had knee surgery and consequently missed spring practice. In the meantime, his backup, Ty Detmer, had a very good spring. In fall camp it became apparent that Ty was going to be our starter. I called Sean in for a talk before I made that decision public. After I'd told him what we were going to do, he thought for a minute and then said, "Coach, I don't think it's fair. I think I deserve to be the starting quarterback. I've been the starter for two years, and now this is a better team than either of those. I know I could win the conference championship with this team."

After having his say, he paused for a minute and then added, "But I want you to know one thing. I want you to know that I'll be at every practice; I'll prepare myself each and every week as if I am going to start. If you ever need me, I'll be ready to go."

And that's exactly what he did. Every game that season he was ready. He practiced every day like he was the starter. He never slowed down, not once, even though Ty Detmer was having one of the greatest sophomore years any quarterback has ever had.

Sean Covey was a great example of one who did what he set out to do no matter what. He acted instead of reacted. He controlled what he could control and dealt with what he couldn't control. He really didn't need the scholarship that year. He had a knee that didn't need any more abuse. There were a lot of reasons he could have used to just walk away. But he was determined to do what he said he would do, and he did. Then he went on to Harvard, got his MBA, and now works with his father and is very successful.

I've spent the bigger part of my life around people like Sean Covey, and I'm that much better off because of it. By associating with people who stretch themselves and are indeed engaged in good causes, who act instead of react, I've been continually inspired myself. My family inspires me, the people I work with inspire me, the players I coach inspire me, the environment I work and live in inspires me. Even the people I compete against inspire me.

I believe God wants us to be actively engaged in good causes, for ourselves and for others. He wants us to stretch ourselves, and for the most part he isn't particular about how we do it. It can be in whatever way we choose. For me, football has been a way to try to stretch myself. It's allowed me to associate in a meaningful way with others, and it's allowed me to develop my own character and discipline. In *Chariots of Fire*, the award-winning movie about the Olympic games, Eric Liddell, the runner from Scotland who refused to run on Sunday, explains to his missionary sister why he trains so hard. He says running is a gift he has been given by God. "When I run," he says, "I can feel his pleasure."

I think that's true for any of us when we choose to expand our God-given talents. When we put forth an honest effort, I think we all can feel God's pleasure. I have very strong feelings about what we've been able to accomplish and how that's had a positive impact on the Church and the university. We've received letters and communications from all parts of the world about BYU football and the role it's played in spreading the gospel.

It would be hard for me to separate my religious beliefs from my beliefs about life in general. My religion is part and parcel of virtually everything I do. I subscribe to the scriptures and to their interpretation by men of God. I believe that the thirteen Articles of Faith, as written by Joseph Smith, the latter-day prophet, are divinely inspired. Starting with the divinity of the Savior and touching on subjects from obedience to tolerance to continuing revelation, they summarize what I believe to be the foundation of Christianity.

I try not to wear what I believe on my cuff. I believe we all have the right to choose for ourselves, and we need to respect that right in others. I do know that my personal beliefs as to the divinity of the Lord Jesus Christ, the sanctity and eternal nature of the family unit, and the importance of listening to Heavenly Father's voice through all of his prophets have enhanced my peace and my happiness. I have no difficulty at all in acknowledging God's hand in everything I do. I only wonder sometimes why I have been so richly blessed.

Friends in Need

Grant Teaff, the president of the American College Football Coaches Association, has known LaVell Edwards since the summer of 1975 when they coached together in an All-Star game in Lubbock, Texas. Since then they have coached together, traveled together, and competed against each other.

"There are brothers who haven't gotten as close as we have," says Teaff. "LaVell and Patti are like family to my wife, Donell, and me. We have a lot in common. You name it, we've done it together."

But of all the things that Patti and LaVell have done for the Teaffs, their greatest gift came in a twelve-hour period of time.

"It was the off season, and as had been our habit for several years, we were looking forward to spending some quality vacation time with LaVell and Patti. As Donell and I winged our way to the island of St. Thomas in the Caribbean, we were envisioning five days of golf and relaxation in the company of our good friends at the Mahogany Run Resort.

"But when we walked in the door we were met with a message from one of our assistant coaches back in Waco, Texas: Our daughter was critically ill with either a brain tumor or a brain hemorrhage. Tammy, our eldest daughter, had been on her way to work on the freeway in Dallas, Texas, and had suddenly lost her sight. Miraculously, she'd gotten off the road and staggered to an apartment door, and someone helped get her to the hospital.

"What was thought to be either a brain tumor or hemorrhage ultimately turned out to be multiple sclerosis. But for several days that diagnosis would not be made. On St. Thomas we were in limbo. We could not leave the island until the next morning. We were in a state that alternated between anxiety and panic.

"Fortunately for us, we were staying in a two-bedroom condominium with the Edwardses.

"They were as upset as we were when they found out about Tammy's condition. They did not leave our side for one moment that night and into the next day. The love and the comfort that they bestowed upon us was so important. We knew that they cared and that they understood how we felt.

"LaVell was always helpful to me in the area of the passing game, and I remember that night, to distract me, we spent two or three hours talking football and drawing up offensive schemes. Even though we were going to play BYU a year later, LaVell shared everything with me. It was not so much the information he gave, but the constant sharing of his spiritual strength and his love that had such a profound impact on me.

"Because of LaVell and Patti, we made it through that night.

"I've said this to anyone who will listen to me: LaVell Edwards is one of the top five coaches to ever coach the game of football. If you don't believe me, just look at his record. But above and beyond that, and of far more importance to me, LaVell Edwards is one of the top five men I've ever known."

CHAPTER TWELVE

Why I Coach

I attended my first national coaching convention in 1962 in Los Angeles. I got in the elevator in the hotel and found myself standing next to Darrell Royal, the legendary Texas coach. He said, "Hello, coach," and I was so nervous I surprised myself when I was able to actually say hello back. I was in awe of the man—and amazed that we both did the same thing for a living.

That feeling has never left me. I've never stopped being surprised that I get to do the same thing as the Darrell Royals, the Woody Hayeses, the Bear Bryants, and the Joe Paternos of this world—that I get to coach.

People ask, "Why do you coach?" Or, lately, "Why do you *continue* to coach?" And my answer is "Why wouldn't I want to coach?" There really is very little about what I do that I don't like. They say you're a lucky man when you get paid for doing what you'd be willing to do for free. They say you're a lucky man when you look forward to going to the office. I'm a lucky man.

I work in a profession that allows a lifestyle compatible with my personal desires. I like the people I work with. I couldn't ask for better working conditions. I love coaching the sport of football. I love the game of college football. I'm in a business that has an abundance of fringe benefits. I'm able to maintain literally thousands of relationships and continually establish new ones. And I've lasted long enough that I've got tenure.

What's not to like?

I've always liked where I live. Utah Valley is where I was born and raised, of course, and I'm sure that has a lot to do with it. I'm comfortable with the lifestyle both in the area and at BYU, and I know that's made my job a lot easier. I'm not at odds, and never have been, with the standards or the policies of the institution I work for. There are certain sensitivities you need when you coach at BYU, and I've never had a problem with any of them. I think that's important if you're going to stay and be content. It's important wherever you are. I know it's had a lot to do with my comfort level over the years. It's had a lot to do with why I've wanted to stay.

I know I'm not the Lone Ranger in that regard. There are a lot of quality people at BYU who could easily leave for excellent positions elsewhere—but they don't want to leave either. That's not publicized too much, but it's true. There are many quality people at BYU, and I enjoy being in that kind of an atmosphere. Nearly everywhere you look here you see people with a sense of wanting to be successful, of wanting to accomplish something. That's very pervasive. Except for me, everyone in my family has earned an undergraduate degree from BYU—Pat got hers in the spring of 1994—and I've always been impressed with how truly accomplished the professors are, with how good they are in working with their students.

I've never worked with a school president I haven't liked, and I'm not sure many football coaches can say that. Ernest Wilkinson, Dallin Oaks, Jeffrey Holland, Rex Lee—they've all been great supporters of BYU football and great supporters of what I've tried to do. I've always had good relationships with the college of physical education and the athletic department. I haven't experienced any of the adversarial relationships that can arise in the competitive world of athletics, the kind of relationships that can take years off your life in huge chunks.

I've been lucky to work with people who don't cut corners, who don't look for loopholes, who don't cheat. I'm particularly proud of that. When I look back on what this program has been able to accomplish, I'm pleased with the number of victories and the records of the quarterbacks and the awards and the trophies—but I'm even more proud of the fact that, whatever we've done, we've done without breaking the rules. We've made football extremely important at BYU, and we've done it fair and square. To my knowledge there has never been an illegal dime given to anybody. That doesn't mean it's never happened. But if it ever has, that's what it's been—a dime. And it was given without my knowledge or approval.

As much as anything—maybe more than anything—I've appreciated the freedom I've had coaching at BYU. It's one of the biggest reasons moving on has never appealed to me. I was never sure that I'd have the same kind of freedom anywhere else. In a place that's viewed as quite restrictive, there's an amazing amount of personal freedom.

I've always felt free to coach and leave it at that. I haven't had to be a fund raiser. I haven't had to run the P.R. department. I haven't been expected to entertain. I'm essentially a private person, and I like nothing more after working in front of 65,000 people on a Saturday afternoon than to go home and spend a quiet evening at home with Pat and maybe a few of the kids who drop by. That's after a win or a loss or a tie, whatever. At BYU I've been able to do that.

I haven't had to spend a lot of time at social gatherings. I haven't had those kinds of obligations. I'm not beholden to a booster club. There aren't four or five key alumni taking care of part of my salary or anything like that. I don't have to look out for those kinds of people. I don't have to hold anyone's hand. I really haven't had any obligations to anybody except my team.

It's not like that everywhere. And I realize some coaches like it that way. There are certainly those coaches who thrive on the social aspects. I've talked to Bobby Bowden, who is a good friend, about what he does at Florida State. Every year in the late spring or summer he and his wife will take a motor home and spend three weeks or a month just traveling around Florida. They'll drive into a place, play a round of golf with some influential boosters, have a cocktail party and dinner that night with the Florida State alumni who live in the area, raise some money, and the next morning move on to another place, where they'll do it all over again.

Bobby likes doing that. I can't think of anything worse. I'd rather take a beating than do that.

I do speak quite a lot—in the off season. I do that because of the Church and BYU, and in the case of clinics, because of the sport. I think back to when I was a young coach and how much I appreciated it when I'd go to a clinic and could listen to someone who had more of a national reputation. A lot of coaches, as they get older and busier, don't do the clinics, and I can understand why. When you have less and less free time, you tend to get more selfish about how you're going to use it. But I do feel a sense of responsibility to the profession.

As for speaking assignments, over the years I've particularly enjoyed meeting people in the outlying areas of the state. I really like the people in small towns. Sometimes Pat and I will get in the car and we'll drive to Vernal or Duchesne or Gunnison or Delta. It's usually not very close. But we'll do that, for a Church fireside or a high school banquet or whatever, and invariably we'll have a good experience. I can speak okay at times and other times not quite as well. I should work at it more. But when I speak I get a sense of satisfaction, a feeling that I'm giving something back. That's why I do it. I've never booked myself with any national agencies to try to make money spending the off season on the speaking circuit. They say Lou Holtz gets $25,000 a speech. I haven't been offered that much yet—for all my speeches combined.

THINGS I LOVE ABOUT COACHING

Coaching football has always been rewarding enough for me in and of itself. I like the teaching aspect of coaching. I like the analytical aspect. I like sizing up a team and deciding what your personnel is going to let you do. I've always liked the competition and I suppose I always will. I know it will be that part that's hardest for me to ever leave.

Coaching has given me the opportunity to experience the whole range of emotions, from the "thrill of victory" to the "agony of defeat"—sometimes in the space of just a few minutes. There is no better example of that than the Holiday Bowl game of 1980, when we beat Southern Methodist University 46–45 in the so-called Miracle Bowl. For most of the night we were just getting pummeled. I remember standing on the sidelines in the middle of the third quarter and thinking, Man, I just hope I never have to go to another bowl game. We'd lost to Indiana in the Holiday Bowl the year before—in what I think was the toughest loss I ever had as a college coach—and at that point we were zero for four in bowl games, soon, I was sure, to be zero for five.

SMU couldn't decide whether to run Eric Dickerson or Craig James at us.

I honestly believed we'd never win a bowl game.

Then on the last play Jim McMahon threw the ball half the length of the field and Clay Brown caught it while surrounded by half the SMU team and we pulled it out. I felt not only the sheer joy of winning—which was enormous—but also the sheer relief of getting a huge monkey off my back. I'll never forget the feeling I had that night.

You're always learning in coaching, and that's an aspect of the profession I've always appreciated. You can't get in a rut and stay there. Well, you can, but it's not advisable. You won't last if you do. We've learned a lot from our losses over the years. The New Mexico game in 1980 is a good case in point. Jim McMahon was starting at quarterback for us that year, taking over from Marc Wilson, who hadn't lost a single regular season game the year before. Our first game was in Albuquerque, where we lost to New Mexico, 25–21. Afterward, there was a lot of public speculation that the players didn't want to play for Jim, that there was dissension and all of that. None of that was even remotely true. None of what happened was Jim's fault, and he was always extremely popular with his teammates.

What it boiled down to is that New Mexico was smarter than we were. Because it was the season opener, New Mexico had had the luxury of spending the summer preparing for us. They'd studied our films carefully and picked up on a flaw in our pass-blocking scheme. They saw that if they overloaded their pass rush on the weak side of the ball, we didn't have a blocking scheme to counter it. So, basically, that's what they did. All night long they brought four pass rushers in on the weak side—the side opposite from where our tight end was lined up. When our center saw that—and it's the center who calls out the blocking scheme you're going to use—he didn't have anything to say that would stop it. The Lobos did something different, something we'd never seen before. And they beat us.

We went back to Provo and spent the week going over the film. By the next weekend we'd been able to make adjustments to our pass blocking that would compensate for other teams trying the same thing—which of course they did, in virtually every other game we played that year. The satisfying part was that we adjusted quickly enough to win all the rest of our games.

That's the beauty of the game of football. It's always changing, always evolving, and you have to be alert. There are constant moves and counter moves. Week in, week out, you see a lot of the same things, but every now and then you see something you haven't seen before. Another one of those games was against Pittsburgh in 1987. Again, it was the first game of the season, and Pittsburgh had spent the summer working on what they planned to try defensively against us. This was when the 46 defense—also known as the Bear defense because it was invented by Buddy Ryan, who was then with the Chicago Bears—was becoming very popular. Chicago had used it to win the Super Bowl the year before.

Pittsburgh introduced us to the 46, and it wasn't a pleasant experience. We had a hard time getting a pass off and lost by ten points in Provo. But just as with the New Mexico game, after we were able to analyze what had happened, we recovered and made the necessary adjustments so we could counter when teams played the Bear defense against us in the future.

Sometimes it's not just one game we learn from. Sometimes it's an experience over an entire season or over a number of seasons. That was the case in 1978, when I alternated Marc Wilson and Jim McMahon at quarterback. After that season I vowed I'd never do that again. I knew I was a one-quarterback kind of coach, and I knew that alternating quarterbacks couldn't work on any team I coached. It took one bad experience to teach me that lesson.

Coaching has allowed me to assess both my strengths and my weaknesses, personally and professionally. It's allowed me to realize that I've been blessed with a kind of sixth sense, an awareness that allows me to size things up intuitively. Over the years many decisions have been based on intuition, and I've gotten more and more confidence as most of those decisions have turned out well.

COLLEGE BALL

Working in the college atmosphere has suited me. The pro game is great, but I like the diversity of the college game. I like the way you're liable to run into everything from the wishbone to the run-and-shoot to the I-formation during the course of the season. And I love the atmosphere, with the bands, the crowds, the cheerleaders, the alumni. College football gives a fan something stable to identify with. It's where you went to school, or it's in your hometown, or it's the team you've decided to align yourself with. And it's not going to move. You can count on it. I can't begin to remember all the people over the years who've said to me in May or July, "Coach, I can hardly wait till fall"— when football season begins. That's given me as much internal satisfaction as anything—to hear that from people, whether it's in the grocery store or the gas station or wherever: "Coach, I just can't wait till football begins again."

That's when college football is at its best. Game day. In the fall, on Saturday afternoon. That's why I like afternoon games. It doesn't have anything to do with whether night games make it harder to win; it's because it just doesn't get any better than a crisp fall afternoon and a football game in the stadium. Sixty-five thousand people. Tailgate parties, all the pregame talk, the bands, the excitement. To me that's what college football is all about.

I've been fortunate to see the college tradition at some of the sport's most venerable shrines. Game day at Penn State and Alabama and Georgia and the Rose Bowl and Notre Dame, to name a few. To have Provo, Utah, join that list, even as a latecomer, is a great thing.

I like the uniqueness of the college game. I like the idea of bowl games, because they give a lot of different people the chance to celebrate their season. It's a great way to tie into your alumni in another area, and to either keep interest in your program high or to revive that interest.

We've seen the same thing happen at Utah the past few years and with Utah State the year they went to the Las Vegas Bowl. The Aggies had more people to that bowl game than they had at some of their home games.

I remember the early bowl games we went to, and how important they were for our program. I still believe that bowl games ought to be more of a reward than anything. I like the concept that it's a way of recognizing a season well done. But I'm not so naive that I don't realize that's a notion of the past. It's not enough just to go to a bowl anymore; you're also expected to win. I've been slow over the years in recognizing that, and I'm sure that has contributed to less success in the bowls than we would have liked and possibly could have had.

I've never really been in favor of a playoff at the end of the season. To me it makes absolutely no sense to carry football past the bowls and into the second or third week of January. I don't think that's proper. And if you have a round-robin playoff that starts the first of December, like they do in the other NCAA divisions, that means you're going to have to eliminate the bowls and you'll be playing games right through finals. I don't think that's right either. If you talk to the people in those divisions that have December playoffs, they'll tell you it's a tough situation.

I'm not saying college football doesn't need to change with the times, or that it isn't in need of a shot in the arm. I think in some ways it is. But the lack of a playoff for the national championship isn't the problem. Whether you win it by being voted in or in a playoff, there's always going to be just one winner. In a way, the controversy that often goes hand in hand with the polls is good for the sport. It gives people something to talk about all during the season, and then through the winter. When we won it in '84 the controversy, in a way, was the best thing that happened to us. People came out and found out more of what BYU was all about. Some of what was reported was positive, some wasn't, but at least people knew who BYU was. We gained an identity. That's happened with a lot of schools.

No matter how the season is brought to an end, the great and unchanging part of college football is the caliber of the student athlete.

The vast majority play because they want to play, because they genuinely love the game, and because they want to get an education. Coaching people like that makes it easy.

And did I mention the part about summers off?

You don't find coaches talking a lot about it in public—probably because it doesn't help during salary negotiations—but you really can't beat the side benefits. You do have your summers off, and there's always a chance for some kind of travel. Pat and I have been to places all around the world—and coaching has had something to do with practically all of our trips. Contrary to what most people would probably think, and contrary to the general conception of a "coach's wife," Pat doesn't want to see me quit. We probably wouldn't travel more in retirement; we'd travel less. Coaching has been good for both of us.

If you let it, I think coaching can keep you young. There's something about the starts and the stops. At the end of every season I'm ready for a break, and at the start of every season I'm ready for it to begin. I enjoy the off season. I love to play golf. But as much as I talk about golf, by August I'm always ready to get back to football.

A PEOPLE BUSINESS

Much more important than these other side benefits of coaching are the relationships you're able to generate and maintain. The longer you coach the more of these relationships you're able to have. Coaching puts you in a position where you can touch many lives—and where you can be touched by many lives. It's often amazing to me the people I've had an influence on. Years later, sometimes decades later, I'll meet someone who will say they did this or that because of some association we had. To think I could influence others like the coaches of my youth influenced me—or even just a fraction of that—brings me a great deal of satisfaction.

Above all else, college football is a people business. The associations and friendships I've developed with players and coaches over the years are invaluable to me. Some of the closest friends I'll ever have are the people I've competed against. Pat and I have traveled to the corners of the earth with coaches and their wives, usually in search of places to shop and places to golf (the two tend to coexist peacefully). The relationships we've developed over the years are irreplaceable.

I know I've been one of the fortunate ones. I've been able to stay in the same place my entire college career. I'm not sure how many times that's happened, but I know it's not very many. I was able to develop and find my own niche, and that was very important. Starting out as a young high school coach, I remember thinking I wanted to be like George Patton, the famous army general. I wanted to be tough like that. I also wanted to emulate Vince Lombardi, the great Packers coach. I wanted to have his kind of toughness and resolve.

Eventually I realized I couldn't really be a Patton or a Lombardi— and I was able to find my own niche. I discovered that while I was a driven person I really wasn't much of a driver, and to be successful that's the way I needed to coach. My teams needed to reflect my personality, not someone else's. The important thing was that I stay true to myself— and to those who worked with me.

I once read an article about Bear Bryant that really impressed me. It talked about how he was a very flamboyant, outgoing individual who demanded a great deal of those who played for him and worked for him. That intrigued me because I personally knew some of the coaches who worked and played for him, guys like Steve Sloan and Jerry Claiborne, and I knew they have personalities quite different from that. I knew their lifestyles were quite different from Bear Bryant's. But the fact that they were different didn't matter. Those guys would have run through a brick wall for that man. To this day they'd run through a brick wall if he could ask them. He was loyal to them, he treated them with respect, and they idolized him for it. To me that says something about getting along, about coming together from a variety of backgrounds and still banding together. In my estimation that's the essence of coaching.

Another thing about Bear Bryant. He was adaptable. Here's a guy who had one of the better passing programs when he won national championships in the '60s. Then he went to the wishbone and won another national championship. When he finally retired he was using a combination of the I-formation and the wishbone, and he was having success with that. There was a flexibility about him that made him more than just a survivor. I've always wondered if I could do that—make a radical departure when I felt it was necessary. I've hoped I could.

I've never been driven by ego, or winning a Heisman Trophy, or winning another national championship, or beating Utah, for that matter. I've never coached because I wanted to establish some kind of dynasty or a particular kind of image. I've never coached because I've had a desire to be perceived as a nice guy or as not a nice guy. I've coached because it suits me. I've coached because what I suspected when I was eight years old was right: Coaching *would* be a great way for me to go through life. That way I could always stop by football practice on my way home from school. How could it get any better than that?

There are demands, of course, and they have increased over the years. It used to be that you were responsible for wins and losses only. That's still the bottom line, but now you're responsible for graduation, you're responsible for the conduct of your team, and you're basically responsible to know what your players are doing at all hours and all months. It's changed a lot over the years. A coach has to be more than just a coach. I'm not sure that's all good. In a lot of ways it's become a tough, unforgiving business.

I thought it would be those kinds of dynamics that would drive me out. To tell the truth, I never thought I'd last as long as I have. I thought if I made it to sixty that would be plenty. Chris Pella likes to remind me that when I hired him, I told him I wouldn't be around much longer. And that was in 1986. But I turned sixty in 1990 and I didn't even think about getting out. I just shot on by.

It's always been like that. It's gone on a lot longer than I ever thought, but I've never stopped enjoying what I'm doing, so there hasn't been any compelling reason to quit. I haven't lived a remarkable life. But I have lived a remarkably lucky life.

I thought I might get tired of the recruiting but I haven't. I thought I might get tired of the mounting expectations but I haven't. I thought

Pat and I would like to serve a Church mission together, and we still have those thoughts for the future, but not this season.

I also thought I'd like to see if what's worked in Provo could work somewhere else. But that hasn't been compelling enough to make me want to leave, either. And if I wouldn't leave the job in Provo for a quarter of a million dollars to coach the Detroit Lions in the National Football League, why would I want to leave it for a rocking chair on my porch? At least, not if I didn't have to.

For all of the reasons I've detailed in this book, and for others I know I haven't even thought to mention, my affection for coaching has been sustained at a high level over the years. People often tell me that if I'm enjoying myself on the sidelines you'd never know it because I don't smile. But when Karl Tucker said, "LaVell's happy—he just forgot to tell his face," he hit it on the head. I've never *not* enjoyed myself. I've never *not* wanted to coach.

I suppose always perceiving myself as a local guy at Granite High trying to figure out how to make a first down has somehow sustained me as well. I've never stopped hearing footsteps. I've never stopped worrying. I've never stopped subscribing to the notion that if you do something good, then you've got at least three more years before they fire you. As long as I've got three more I'd feel ungrateful not to use them.

I realize I can't coach forever. When it's time to step aside, I'll know it. I'm confident of that. It will be a feeling that it's the right thing to do, and I won't have any problem doing it. It doesn't have to come after any particular event or milestone. When it does happen I'd like to move on, serve a mission, or find some other involvement. I don't want to get involved in athletic administration or become some kind of special assistant to the president or anything like that. I don't want to be in a position where I'm looking over someone's shoulder—or where someone *thinks* I'm looking over his shoulder.

I've always said that when I do retire, that's when I'll have time to stop and reflect on everything that's happened. I've never really thought about any of it very much. But in retirement I'll be able to kick back in a rocking chair and reminisce on the league titles and the bowl games and the All-American quarterbacks and the national championship and the Heisman Trophy and all of that. I'll be able to analyze it all and have a much better idea of how it all happened. I'll be able to give people some better answers. I'll be able to size it all up perfectly.

At least that's what I keep saying. That I'll really think about it then. Even though I know I probably won't.